LANDMARK COLLECTOR'S LIF

THE SPIRIT O
KIRK IRE

Gill Ashurst, Jan Walding & Dave Williams

Thanks for all your help
in moving to this
wonderful place.
Much love,
Justina, Mark + Andrey.

Published by

Landmark Publishing Ltd
Ashbourne Hall, Cokayne Ave, Ashbourne, Derbyshire DE6 1EJ England
Tel: (01335) 347349 Fax: (01335) 347303
e-mail: landmark@clara.net
website: www.landmarkpublishing.co.uk

ISBN 1 84306 148 1

© Gill Ashurst, Jan Walding & Dave Williams 2004

Print: Bath Press, Bath
Design: Mark Titterton
Cover: James Allsopp

Front cover: Barley Mow.

Title page: Well Banks.

Back cover top: Pupils with teacher Miss Jessie Archer.

Back middle: Millennium photograph.

Back cover bottom: Wakes procession in 1949/1950.

LANDMARK COLLECTOR'S LIBRARY

THE SPIRIT OF
KIRK IRETON

Gill Ashurst, Jan Walding & Dave Williams

Landmark Publishing

Contents

Introduction

Imagine a map of Great Britain. Draw on it two lines, one due west from the most northerly point of the Norfolk coast, the other due north from the Needles (the most westerly point of the isle of Wight). The intersection of these two lines lies less than two miles from the Derbyshire village of Kirk Ireton.

This village has been a place of human habitation since the Bronze Age, a fact to which numerous small Bronze Age burial sites and artifacts bear witness. Despite its elevated position overlooking the lower Derwent and Trent valleys, on reasonable farming ground, well watered, and with resources of gritstone, sand and gravel within its parish boundaries, the village has for centuries had a population of around 400. This stability is primarily due to this number being all that the land could support and also to the difficulties of approaching it compared with surrounding villages. Idridgehay, on the way to Wirksworth, lying some 300 feet below it in the Ecclesbourne Valley was chosen for a 19th century rail route towards the north, whilst Hognaston to the west, beyond the marshy area which is now Carsington Reservoir, was one of the main Derby – Manchester road routes.

The ridge between the two, on which Kirk Ireton stands, was used by the Romans, probably as part of their Chester – Chester Green (Derby) road, but this route fell out of favour.

Today the number of people engaged in farming, once the predominant industry, is small and most of the working population travel to Derby and other local towns for employment. Despite the influx of 'outsiders' following the installation of mains services (still excluding gas) and widespread car ownership in the post war years, families whose roots go back numerous generations still comprise a significant minority of the population.

Today Church, Chapel, Village Hall, school and pub (now reduced to the solitary Barley Mow) provide the hub of village activities.

Acknowledgement

Kirk Ireton Local History Group was formed in 1985 with the aim of preserving whatever was of historical interest relating to the village. This included not only gathering physical evidence, but also interviewing and recording the recollections of older inhabitants. Three of the original members who still live in the village have collated the work of the Group in this book. They would like to thank previous members for their contribution, but in particular the people of Kirk Ireton; without their contributions there would be little of interest to recall here. Whenever asked, they have been generous with their time in sharing their memories and in lending personal papers and pictures. There is insufficient space to list all those who have contributed, but we hope they think we have made good use of their contributions. Also thanks to the Ashbourne News Telegraph for the use of their pictures.

We have attempted to ensure that all the detail in this book is correct. We apologise if it is thought that errors have been made.

Shops and Other Occupations

Farming was the main source of employment in the village for centuries, but some other occupations have been followed for many years and the number of these alternatives has increased markedly during the last century. It is probable that butchery, closely aligned with farming, was the first of these but not, originally, as a full-time occupation.

It is very probable that the occupation of carpenter was practised very early on but this would not initially have involved making coffins as most people were buried in shrouds.

Clergyman is certainly the oldest occupation not directly involved with farming. It must be remembered, however, that part of the clergyman's salary was in the form of tithes, so even he was not entirely without dependence on the land.

It was not until the 17th century that influences outside the village began to have an impact on the employment of villagers, this was when some ale houses became inns and 'publican' became an occupation, catering for passing travellers as well as villagers.

The 19th century saw the first full time headmaster and the first income independent of farming. Female teachers followed before the end of the century, as did a postmaster and postmen although these latter were either augmenting a farming living or adding to a post office income by farming.

Quarry work was available, first in the gritstone quarries, and subsequently in Blackwall's sand and gravel, quarries.

Woodcutters largely travelled to Durham and Gloucestershire for their work which was also associated with the making of clogs from alder wood.

There was employment in shops. These were either of a general nature or specialists such as dressmakers or cobbler/shoe makers. One enterprising cobbler also used his cobbling pincers in the part-time occupation of dentist and, as another sideline, dug wells for farmers.

At this time the village had its own village constable and a road repairer, the latter continuing until mid 20th century.

There were employment opportunities in domestic service; these were mainly for females but also included gardeners and footmen.

One person, Matilda Powles, perhaps better known as 'Vesta Tilley', was a theatrical performer and at the end of the 19th century the village, for a decade, had its own resident artist, George Turner, sometimes referred to as 'The Derbyshire Constable'.

The 20th century, in which both personal transport and mains services became widely available, saw a huge increase in workers who live in the village but work in local towns or other villages; these have included architects, doctors, scientists, solicitors and teachers, as well as persons who run, or work for, businesses which could not have been remotely imagined at the start of the 20th century.

The Post Office

In many towns and cities the post offices are purpose built. This has not generally been the case in our villages, consequently it is not unusual to find that the location of the post office, which has often been the home of the current postmaster, has moved around following the resignation, retirement or death of the post holder.

This has been the case in Kirk Ireton. The post of 'receiver' was first advertised in September 1852 and the date shown on the first franking stamp was later in that year. In 1853 the post was again advertised following the resignation of the holder. This time the vacancy was filled by George Ford of Rose Cottage, Nether Lane. George retired due to ill health in 1870 and his wife Elizabeth, who had been running the office for some time, took over. Elizabeth ran the office until 1891 when she retired at the age of 83.

Mrs Selina Smedley of Greenbank, opposite the church, was the next office holder. Considerable changes took place during her tenure; in 1896 the number of deliveries was increased to three a week, in 1897 the office became a Money Order Office and two years later deliveries were again increased, this time to six a week. 1899 also saw the introduction of the 'Telegraph' allowing telegrams to be received and sent from the post office; it has been recorded that sometimes the office was closed while telegrams were delivered to outlying farms.

The Old Post Office, Main Street. This was the site of the Post office around 1910
when Evelyn Dean was the postmistress.

Various postmarks used when post was franked in the village.

Miss Evelyn Dean took over the office in 1910 and the office moved to the junction of Coffin Lane and Main Street, now Derwent House.

It is important to remember that up to this time there was no motor transport and the mail was generally collected and delivered on foot. The following recollection is of interest:-

'You could hear him going about 5 am, walking down (*to Idridgehay*). He'd fetch the mail, load up with parcels, walk up to Ireton, sort it and deliver it, even to Callow and Biggin. Then in the afternoon he'd go round again and take it down to Idridgehay and put it on the train.'

Miss Dean (later Mrs Simpson) administered the office until 1944. A Mr. Greatorex, followed by his son Billy, made the deliveries during the earlier years and later it is recorded that:-

'Frank Sherwin, of Prospect Cottage on The Flatts, helped Billy Greatorex part time, 'cos he was a farmer' Later 'Johnny Sherwin shared the round with Ada Hodgkinson, he delivered to the bottom of the village, she covered the outlying farms because she was younger and biked it. At Christmas it took all three of them to carry it.'

Doris Linthwaite became sub-postmistress in 1944 so, after a break of 15 years, the Post Office returned to Greenbank, her home. Doris continued as sub-postmistress until her retirement in 1988 aged 87. Post was not franked in the village after 1976.

Briefly the office moved to a shop at the corner of Hemp Yard and Main Street with the Cromacks running it, but this shop closed and for a short while the village had neither a shop nor a post office.

Soon, however, a community based project opened a temporary shop in the garage of Rose Bank Cottage on Hemp Yard. The GPO allowed an office to be set up in this with Mrs Kate Spencer as postmistress.

The village shop was re-established in 1990, on the corner of Hemp Yard and Main Street, with Mrs Margaret Varney as post mistress. This establishment closed in 2001 when Mrs Varney retired and once again the village was without these two essential assets; however Mrs Mary Short, the landlady of The Barley Mow, provided the present premises, in a converted stable adjoining the pub, to which the shop moved in 2001 and the post office a little later.

The picture has the legend 'Sheffield Telegraph. By the village carrier, Kirk Ireton.'

Greenbank Cottage. In 1849 William Smedley ran a bakery in the premises. By 1881 the business was run by his son George. It is recalled he delivered bread to Idridgehay using a donkey with panniers for transport. After visiting Idridgehay he would return to Kirk Ireton via Ireton Wood. Subsequently the building became the site of the Post Office run by Mrs Doris Linthwaite for 43 years.

Doris Linthwaite on the occasion of her 100th birthday visited by the local school children and their teacher, Kate Varley.

September Cottage, Main Street

There has been a shop in this location intermittently from as early as 1829, when James Poyser, described as Shopkeeper and Maltster, lived on the premises. Samuel Dean occupied the cottage as a grocer and draper at the time of the 1881 census.

The Clay family moved into the village in the 1880s and there were three generations of Clay shopkeepers – Harriet from the 1890s, Ernest from 1904 and Alfred from 1957. Initially their shop was sited across the road.

Harriet was renowned for making her own black puddings, using pigs reared on the premises. She washed the 'chitterlings' at Pearl Well Farm.

Ernest ran the shop for over 50 years, as well as performing other duties such as Parish Clerk and Tax Collector.

Alfred Clay took over the shop in 1957, after working as a baker in Hognaston. Mr Clay is well remembered by many in the village. He sold a wide variety of merchandise: boots, shoes, drapery, and ironmongery as well as foodstuffs and newspapers. Some delicacies were prepared on the premises, notably hams cooked in water paste (which attracted people from miles around).

Buxton House, Main Street. Original site of Clay's shop.

The outside of Clay's shop circa 1965.

10

Christmas and wedding cakes were made to order and were excellent! Items that were requested but not kept in stock were ordered and collected specially from Derby.

On the 23rd of February 1957 the shop was held up by a 16-year-old boy carrying a Browning pistol. After he was given 9s 6d he tried to escape on a bicycle but Mrs Clay pushed him off. He was eventually caught running across a field.

In 1974 Marie Whitehurst took over the shop. Hams were still cooked on the premises and continued to attract customers from afar. The shop ceased trading in 1979.

Alfred and Mildred Clay inside their shop. Examples of items sold: Blancmange powders; Barley flakes; Pearl barley; Essences; Figs; Gravy salts; Fish and meat pastes; Tapioca; Tobacco; Ammonia; Waterglass; Bird seed and bird sand; Blues (Dolly); Creams (Dolly); Candles; Electric lamps; Tapers; Coffee (essence) and homemade Lollipops.

At one time, the building on the right was a Smithy run by Isaac Beeston. His wife ran a small business selling paraffin, nails, boots, shoes, and general hardware. These goods were displayed in the side window opposite the school. In the 1930s shoe prices ranged from 3/6d to 5/- per pair. Paraffin was about 4d per gallon.

Mrs Annie Bates who lived with her mother in the school house opposite, remembers watching the horses being shod and the cartoon which hung inside the shop of an old man and woman in bed.

'Get up wife 'tis washing day,
No, Rinso has been washing whilst we slept!'

Beeston's shop 1919.

Grocery order
book from 1947.

After the death of Mrs Beeston the Smithy was sold to Wirksworth and District Co-Operative Society for £1000.00. (Prior to this the Co-op existed in the village in the dwelling since named Briar Cottage.) It was then refurbished and existed as the Co-op from 1948-1967. Sam Bowyer worked there, and was manager in 1951. Various other people were sent from the Wirksworth branch to run the shop, including Mrs B Ford, Chris Else and the last manager was George Taylor.

Older villagers recall butter and lard sold from barrels or butter cut from a slab and sugar sold loose from sacks. Customers would take linen bags to collect a 'stone' of flour. Tea was bought by the quarter and coffee was a luxury, sold in the form of beans – usually bought by "those who lived at the Rectory" for example.

Milk was sold at 2d a pint, from a bucket, but most villagers collected their milk from the local farms, particularly Green Farm. A Mr Naylor was the milkman from Kniveton but he used to break down regularly and often didn't arrive until 3 p.m!

From 1968 Bert and Edith Hallows managed The Corner Shop until 1984 when the shop was renamed Kirk Ireton Food and Wine Store under the ownership of John Smith and later the Cromack family.

When the Cromacks left there was the possibility that, for the first time, the village would be without a shop. In the space of ten days the villagers found premises (the garage belonging to Rosebank Cottage), raised £4,500 for staff and stock and conversion costs, obtained Post Office and Local Authority clearance and opened for business. The shop operated until the Food and Wine Store was sold to the Varney family.

The inside of the 'Garage Shop' with post mistress Kate Spencer on the right, shop assistant Claire Cudworth on the left.

In 2001 the Varneys ceased trading. Realising the possibility of the village losing these facilities altogether Mary and Tony Short converted part of their stable block at the Barley Mow to accommodate the shop and Post Office.

Rosebank Cottage, Hemp Yard

Above: Samuel Sherwin and his son Alan ran a Joiners and Undertakers business on this site from the 1890s until the 1950s, taking over from Thomas Holmes.

The site boasted a long shed for timber storage and an enormous sawing pit. Using a very large saw Sam Sherwin, with his son below in the pit, would saw locally hewn trees.

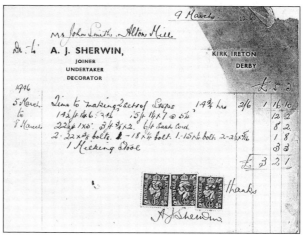

Right: An example of a bill issued by the Sherwins.

Above: The sawpit at
Rosebank Cottage.

Above and right: A selection
of tools used by the
Sherwins.

To this day Samuel Sherwin's work can be admired in Holy Trinity Church, where he made the pews, altar rails and pulpit. The latter was crafted in memory of Benjamin Abell's son, Henry, who was killed, aged 18, in the First World War. The oak for the pulpit was given by General Walthall of the Alton Manor Estate.

In 1932 the Prince of Wales paid a visit to Alan Sherwin's workshop to inspect work that Alan had made for the Rural Community Council. Some of the older villagers recall the visit but despite hearty renderings of 'God Bless The Prince Of Wales,' from the school playground, the children felt they were hardly acknowledged!

From the school logs of 2 June 1932: 'Lessons disorganised today owing to Prince of Wales' visit to Kirk Ireton at 2:00 p.m. until 3:10 p.m. when the Prince left. After this with the Chairman's permission the school was dismissed'.

The Prince of Wales in Hemp Yard with Mr Storer leaning over the gate.

Briar Cottage

James Simpson used this building as a butcher's shop around 1870. He was the father of Lillian Ford who was the licensee of the Barley Mow for many years. The slaughterhouse was across the road in what is now Churchside Cottage. Briar Cottage became a general store and bakery with its bake-house on Coffin Lane. Customers could take their own bread and cakes for baking there.

In 1926 Briar cottage became a branch of the Wirksworth and District Co-operative Society. By 1947 the premises had become very run down and it was ordered that the shop be closed. It was said that passers-by could see the lard in the window being eaten by rats.

Rose Cottage, Nether Lane

It is recorded in September 1852 that there was a vacancy for a receiver in the village. As the first hand stamp was issued in November 1852 there must have been a Post Office in the village by that time. A directory from 1855 shows George Ford as the sub-postmaster. The mail came from Wirksworth at 10:15 a.m. and was sent out at 4:30 p.m. Mrs Ford took over as sub-postmistress in 1884 and retired in 1891.

By 1890 the post was arriving in the village via Idridgehay.

Northfield Farm...the shop

This shop was built on the Main Street at the turn of the century. It used to be a beer store when Stanley Dean's father, Isaac Dean was alive. The beer came from Alton's Brewery in Burton. Stanley's father used the premises to store ale, and he travelled around outlying farms selling beer from a horse and cart. 'The days he was out delivering beer were red letter days for the kids because they used to roll the barrels right down Stanley's drive, and a bloke stood there with a great big bag of corn, stopping them.'

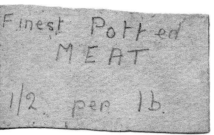

Stanley Dean later used the building as a butcher's shop. He had a licence to slaughter – with the slaughterhouse in the outbuilding behind Northfield Farm. Stanley's sisters Alice, Lizzie and Annie, helped to run the shop, making potted meat and ice-cream.

Left: Sign found under the floorboards of Northfield Farm.

19

The Smithy, Moor Lane

Records show a 'Malt Office' on this site in 1846. George Wright was recorded as a blacksmith here before 1881 and the Smithy remained in the Wrights-Roper family for over 100 years. Tom Sutton took over the business in 1938 and finished working in 1955. The present bungalow was built on the site about 45 years ago.

It is recalled that during Albert Jesse Roper's time as blacksmith, for one week of the year no shoeing took place. Extra workers were taken on for "whooping" the many wooden carts of the village. Boy's hoops were made during that week too.

Bill issued by Tom Sutton.

Holly Bush Farm (Now Kismet Cottage) Main Street

During recollections of their childhood (1920s) Luke Wood and John Jennings remembered two fish and chip shops in Kirk Ireton. One was sited here, run by Mrs Oliver.

Main Street.

Sunnyside, Main Street

In 1850 shoemaker Michael Hoon, and later his son George lived here. George Hoon was almost as renowned for removing teeth, as he was for repairing shoes. It is said he used the same pincers for both jobs.

Elsie Ward recalled a tale told by her Granny, who suffered at the hands of Hoon's pliers. Having had the offending tooth removed and after rinsing her mouth into his bucket, the intoxicated Hoon claimed loudly that all his water had turned red!

The Cottage, Main Street

Arthur and his brother Daniel Doxey were builders and stonemasons. Arthur rebuilt a low stone house originally on this site into the 'Cottage' as it stands today. There are many testimonies to their work still in evidence in the village, including the Church (now Village) Institute, the Rectory, and the Primitive Methodist Chapel. Arthur was a monumental mason and many of the headstones in the churchyard were carved by him.

2. Church and Chapel

Holy Trinity Church looking North-West.

Everyone, we are told, can be famous for 15 minutes. So too, it seems, can buildings. Kirk Ireton's Holy Trinity Church's time came in 1994 when it was viewed all over the country in the TV drama *Peak Practice* when Dr Jack Kerruish (Kevin Whately) married Dr Beth Glover (Amanda Burton) there.

It was perhaps a strange choice of church to make for the wedding for, despite its grand and solid exterior, there is one interior feature which does cramp wedding ceremonies, a step down from the nave to the chancel. Most churches have a step up, or remain level at this point. It is thought that the nave has been raised over the years to accommodate changes to the ground level outside the church; ground level on the south side of many churches has tended to rise as the southern side has been favoured for burials. Another, darker, explanation might be that skeletons, formerly in the graveyard, have been reburied in the church; something which has occurred in many other churches and which appears to the reason for the many skeletons found beneath the floor of the church at nearby Mugginton. It should perhaps be remembered that there have been burials here at least since 1120 and that there are less than 300 graves in the churchyard; some, admittedly, family ones.

No evidence for a Saxon church has been found on the site; the oldest, barn like structure appears to date from about 1120 and the lower portion of the tower, nave, aisles and south door are all dated between 1120 and 1170. At this time the interior must have been dark; the tower had only a small low window and there were probably only a few similar windows in the aisles.

The church was extended to the east during the 14th century by the addition of a chancel. Other additions at this time included a porch at the south door, a vestry on the northern side of the chancel, and a bell chamber, giving greater height to the tower. An additional door, on the north side, opposite the existing one was pierced during this period. This has since been filled in but its outline may still be seen. It should also be noted that the present south door and the door into the tower, from the body of the church, result from the partial in-filling of older Norman arches. Both arches are still visible.

It was apparently not until the 15th century and 16th century that the interior of the church was made lighter; work was undertaken to extend the aisles along both sides of the chancel. More windows resulted from this but increasing the overall height of the walls by topping them with a clerestory (a wall containing an area of windows) running the length of the nave, was probably even more effective. Raising the walls would also require the roof to be raised, but evidence for roof changes (from steep pitched thatch to flattened lead) can only be dated to 1674; a date cast into the lead of the roof. This roof was replaced in 1973.

The most significant changes of the 18th and 19th centuries concerned the tower. As mentioned above, the alteration to the Norman arch to the tower was made, and three bells were added to a small (presumed) Sanctus bell. Other changes during this period involved the removal of the boxed pews from the nave and a gallery from the church tower end of the nave. Musicians may have used the gallery, in the days prior to the installation of an organ, as described by Thomas Hardy in some of his novels. The large stained glass window at the east end of the chancel, in memory of members of the Blackwall family, dates from 1886.

There are two fonts, the most recent, in memory of Rev. Robert Gell, and its predecessor, a pedestal font. The original Norman font was destroyed when a workman used it as a vessel in which to melt lead.

A certain amount of detective work and deduction can be enjoyed when looking at small features around both the interior and exterior of the church; small brackets, for chandeliers or oil lamps are present and also some window catches. There are only two monuments, a small brass plaque of 1572 written in Latin in the northern aisle, and a stone one, dated 1663, behind the altar. The original altar table, bearing the legend 'Thomas Heywood 1679' is now in the south aisle. Perhaps of greater interest are the details of the various charities to do with the village, which are to be seen in the tower.

The Church looking North.

In May 1811 a tornado ripped off the tower roof and the iron reinforcing framework, to be seen just below the clock, is a direct result of the remedial actions found necessary after this event. The door was once used as the access to the gallery.

One of the crude faces on the south chancel door.

The gates have 18th century gate piers reputedly originally from the Manor House, which was on the site of the present school.

Left: The vestry door described as 'almost unique' with four-leafed flowers carved within the arch. It is rare to find a vestry in a pre-Reformation church.

Below: The porch, added in the 14th century.

Early pictures of the interior of the Church showing both Norman and 14th century arches.

Right: The Church
Seal from 1821.

Below: The seating plan from the redesigning
of the interior of the Church in 1872/3.

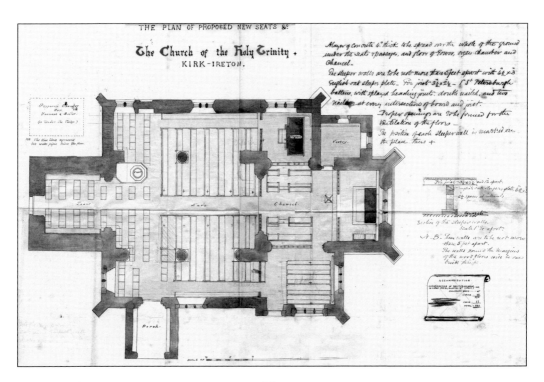

Details of Kirk Ireton Charities 1899.

Opposite page: Cover for the Order of Services celebrating the re-opening of the Church on 24 September 1873.

KIRK IRETON

THE

Church of the Holy Trinity,

AT

KIRK IRETON,

WILL BE

RE-OPENED

ON

WEDNESDAY, SEPTEMBER THE 24TH, 1873.

Services.

Holy Communion at 8 a.m.

Morning Service at 11.

Sermon by the Lord Bishop of Lichfield.

Afternoon Service at 3 p.m.

Sermon by the Right Reverend Bishop Abraham.

COLLECTIONS

in aid of the Restoration Fund will be made at Morning and Afternoon Services.

(OVER)

SLATER'S, COOPER'S, AND HUTCHINSON'S CHARITIES.

Rev. John Slater left Five Closes of Land, now producing a rental of £40 per annum, of which £8 per annum is to be paid to the Teachers of Kirk Ireton Schools, for the education of sixteen children of the poorest inhabitants, the remainder, £32, to be given by the Minister and Church-wardens to the poor inhabitants of the parish at Midsummer and Christmas.

Robert Cooper, of Thurstfield, left the land called "Sidewood," the rents arising therefrom, £14 10s. 0d., to be paid to poor housekeepers and widows.

John Hutchinson left Two Fields called "Pearl Flat," and "Ferny Croft," the rents arising therefrom, £1 per annum, to be distributed to the poor at Midsummer and Christmas.

The interest of money derived from the sale of timber grown on the lands devised by Rev. John Slater, and Robert Cooper, amounting last year to £17 8s. 2d., is also distributed among the poor of Kirk Ireton at Midsummer and Christmas. These sums amount altogether to £72 18s. 2d.; deducting from this £8 for the use of the Schools, leaves a balance of £64 18s. 2d., which was distributed last year as follows :—

DISTRIBUTED AT MIDSUMMER, 1871.

Persons		s.	d.	£	s.	d.
2 Persons	at	20	0	2	0	0
1	"	19	0	0	19	0
3	"	18	0	2	14	0
3	"	17	0	2	11	0
2	"	16	0	1	12	0
1	"	15	0	0	15	0
5	"	14	0	3	10	0
3	"	13	0	1	19	0
5	"	12	0	3	0	0
2	"	11	0	1	2	0
3	"	10	0	1	10	0
5	"	9	0	2	5	0
3	"	8	0	1	4	0
6	"	7	0	2	2	0
4	"	6	0	1	4	0
1	"	5	7	0	5	7
5	"	5	0	1	5	0
4	"	4	0	0	16	0
1	"	3	9	0	3	9
3	"	3	0	0	9	0
3	"	2	0	0	6	0
Fencing				0	7	6
Expense of Charity Commissioners returns				0	10	0
				£32	9	10

DISTRIBUTED AT CHRISTMAS, 1871.

Persons		s.	d.	£	s.	d.
4 Persons	at	20	0	4	0	0
2	"	18	0	1	16	0
3	"	17	0	2	11	0
2	"	16	0	1	12	0
1	"	15	0	0	15	0
5	"	14	0	3	10	0
3	"	13	0	1	19	0
6	"	12	0	3	12	0
2	"	11	0	1	2	0
1	"	10	0	0	10	0
1	"	9	6	0	9	6
4	"	9	0	1	16	0
3	"	8	0	1	4	0
6	"	7	0	2	2	0
5	"	6	0	1	10	0
1	"	5	7	0	5	7
6	"	5	0	1	10	0
2	"	4	0	0	8	0
1	"	3	9	0	3	9
3	"	3	0	0	9	0
3	"	2	0	0	6	0
Fencing				0	7	6
Expense of Charity Commissioners returns				0	10	0
				£32	8	4

The names of the persons who have received the above-mentioned sums are entered in the Churchwardens' book, and may be seen on application to Mr. Harvey.

Details of Slater Cooper and Hutchinson's Charities. The village has had the benefit of up to seven charities, some established as far back as the late 16th century.

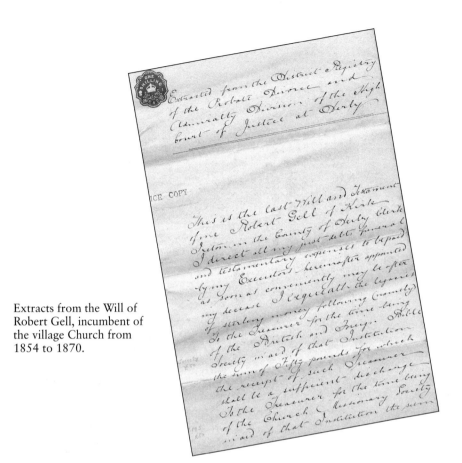

Extracts from the Will of Robert Gell, incumbent of the village Church from 1854 to 1870.

Extracted from the District Registry of the Probate Divorce and Admiralty Division of the High Court of Justice at Derby

ICE COPY

This is the last Will and Testament of me Robert Gell of Kirk Ireton in the County of Derby Clerk I direct all my just debts funeral and testamentary expenses to be paid by my Executors hereafter appointed as soon as conveniently may be after my decease I bequeath all the legacies of sterling money following (namely) To the Treasurer for the time being of the British and Ir…… …ille… Society in aid of that Institution the sum of Fifty pounds for which the receipt of such Treasurer shall be a sufficient discharge To the Treasurer for the time being of the Church Missionary Society in aid of that Institution the sum

discharge To the Official Trustees of Charitable Funds in England and Wales the sum of Five hundred pounds to be by them invested and settled in such manner so that the annual interest arising therefrom may for ever hereafter from time to time as and when the same shall be received be paid to or for the benefit of the Schoolmaster for the time being of the Free School in Kirk Ireton aforesaid in augmentation of his salary To Daniel Pickering of Kirk Ireton aforesaid School

32

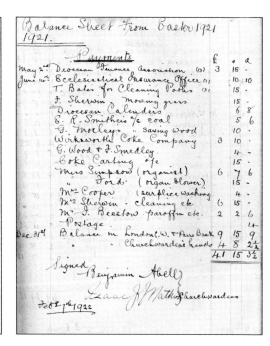

The Institute. Maintenance.

RECEIVED.		£ s. d.	PAID.		£ s. d.
I. The Club.			I. The Club.		
1910. Oct. to Dec. Old Room.			1910. Rent of old room, 14 w'ks		14 0
Boys' Subscriptions	...	3 3½	Coal for do.	...	15 10
Mens' do.	...	10 6	1911. Darts, Bazique marker,		
1911. Jan. to Mar. New Room.			Cards	...	5 7½
Boys' Subscriptions	...	4 11	II. The Club and General Purposes.		
Mens' do.	...	1 3 0	Caretaker, three months		1 10 0
II. General Purposes.			Coal and Coke	...	1 10 1
1911. Opening tea, net	...	8 6	Oil for lamps	...	16 0½
Lectures	...	3 7			
Dance 5/-, Whist Drive 5/-	...	10 0			
Donation by Rector	...	2 7 9½			
		£5 11 7			£5 11 7

Kirk Ireton School Building Fund, 1910.

RECEIVED.		£ s. d.	PAID.		£ s. d.
Brought forward Jan. 1st, 1910	26 15 9		Wear and Tear to Local		
Hire of Room for Political,			Authority	...	2 12 9
Social, and other purposes	3 5 0		Fire Insurance	...	4 9
Rent of School House	...	4 10 0	Rates and Taxes	...	1 5 4
Downing Charity	...	3 0 0	Mr. Wood for attending to		
Grant from endowment for use			School Yard	...	5 0
of Managers	...	5 0 0	Mr. A. Doxey, for repairs	...	3 0
			Diocesan affiliation fee	...	5 0
			Mr. Beeston, for oil	...	1 13 0
			Mr. Hoon, for carting	...	4 0
			Bibles for use in School	...	18 0
					7 10 10
			Brought forward Dec. 31st, 1910		34 19 11
		£42 10 9			£42 10 9

Kirk Ireton Church School Endowment, 1910.

RECEIVED.		£ s. d.	PAID.		£ s. d.
Brought forward	...	34 10 0	School Library.		
Jan. 10, Charity Commissioners		6 3 11	Jan. 26th, Books	...	3 14 7
April 9, do. do.		6 3 11	Feb. 2nd, Printing Catalogues...		13 6
June 30, Bank Interest	...	6 0	Prices.		
July 9, Charity Commissioners		6 3 11	June 7th, In the form of clothes:		
October 10, do. do.		6 3 11	July 20, Land 17/-, Clay £4,		
Bank Interest	...	6 0	Beeston 11/-, Ward 32/-...		7 0 0
			School Gardens.		
			Medal 7/6, Seeds 16/4,		
			Manure 10/-, Roses 4/-		1 17 10
			School Managers', Grant	...	5 0 0
					18 5 11
			Balance carried forward		41 11 9
		£59 17 8			£59 17 8

Kirk Ireton Parish Magazine.

Vol. I. No. 7.   JULY, 1913.   Price 1d.

Services at the Parish Church.

SUNDAYS: Holy Communion, 8 a.m.; on the 3rd Sunday, at 10 a.m.
Matins and Sermon 10-45 a.m. Evensong and Sermon 6-30 p.m.
On last Sunday in the month, Service for children, with address, 2 p.m.
On last Sunday in month, second celebration of Holy Communion after Matins.
Preparation Service for Holy Communion, on last Sunday in month, after Evensong.
SAINTS' DAYS: On the Eve, Evensong 6-30. Holy Communion, 8 a.m.; Evensong, 6-30.
Notice will be given of all Special Services during the seasons of Advent and Lent.
The Sacrament of Holy Baptism will be administered on any week-day evening after notice has been given,
and on the 1st Sunday in every month at 2-30 p.m.
Churchings will be taken any time, after notice has been given.
A Short Address will be given at Holy Communion on the 2nd Sunday in the month.
Funerals (except under special circumstances) at 3-30 p.m. from October 1st to April 1st, and at 4-30 p.m. from
April 1st to October 1st.
The Church will be open at all times throughout the year, for private prayer.
Daily Prayer (Matins) at 8 a.m. all the year round.

Church Officers.

Rector: REV. R. STEWART HARE, M.A.
Churchwardens: John B. Evans-Blackwall, Esq., Blackwall, Kirk Ireton; Mr. Joseph Matkin, Kirk Ireton.
Sidesmen: Messrs. B. Abell, Isaac Beeston. Isaac Dean, A. Dransfield, S. S. Sherwin, and W. Simpson.
Organist: Miss Simpson. *Parish Clerk:* The Rector. *Deputy Clerk, Sacristan, and Caretaker of the Church:* Mr. S. S.
Sherwin. *Sexton:* Mr. John Smedley.
Choir Practices: For Boys only, in Church Institute, Wednesdays, 3 or 4 p.m. (according to season). Full Practice
in Church, Wednesdays, 7-30.
Meeting for Members of Mothers' Union: Every Wednesday at 2 p.m. (Church Institute).
"King's Messengers" on Saturday, at 2-30 p.m. (Church Institute).
Edited by the Rector of Kirk Ireton, to whom all communications must be addressed.   Printed by A. Barker & Sons, Wirksworth.

Above: *Parish Magazine* cover from July 1913.

Above left: Kirk Ireton Parochial Report of 1911. Above right: A page from the Church Accounts book 1921.

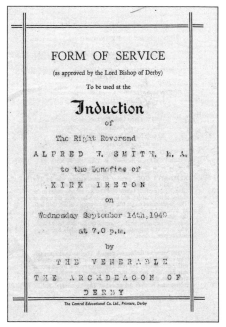

FORM OF SERVICE

(as approved by the Lord Bishop of Derby)

To be used at the

Induction

of

The Right Reverend

ALFRED W. SMITH, M.A.

to the Benefice of

KIRK IRETON

on

Wednesday September 14th, 1949

at 7.0 p.m.

by

THE VENERABLE

THE ARCHDEACON OF

DERBY

The Central Educational Co. Ltd., Printers, Derby

Above: Induction of Rev.(Bishop) Alfred W. Smith. He had been a Bishop in Nigeria before coming to the village. While returning to this country the ship on which his wife was travelling was bombed and sunk by the Luftwaffe and she is said to have landed with only the keys to her luggage.

The Book of Common Prayer being performed in Church late 1930s. The Church has hosted various productions over the years. Older villagers recall *The Book Beloved* which was performed in the late 1930s. It was written by Mrs Gell of Hopton Hall and depicted different services from the Prayer Book. The production lasted over two hours and was performed in the churches at Hognaston and Cromford as well as Kirk Ireton. Funds raised went to the Cathedral Fund.

Tea being taken at a Rectory Garden Party in the late 1940s. Those present include: Elizabeth Smedley, Ethel Greatorex, Elizabeth and Harold le Grice, Elsie Ward and Ellen Smith.

Mrs Gell being presented with a bouquet at a Rectory Garden Party in the early 1950s. From left to right: Bishop Smith, Mrs Gell, Margaret Ward, Mark Hallows, Mrs Bishop Smith; and Mrs Pat Blackwall, Miss Millicant Blackwall and Miss Gregory who helped to look after the Rectory. The group in the background are: Lucy Cooper, Stanley Cooper, Mrs Adlington and Mrs Abell.

Taken on the lawn at the Rectory in the early 1950s. Back row left to right: Edward Masson, Alan Sherwin, Mrs Smedley, Alice Sherwin, Ena Matkin, Marion Dean, Lizzie Dean and Mr Wain.
Front row left to right: Mrs Smith, Rev.(Bishop) Smith, Mrs Walthall, General Walthall, Mrs Blackwall, Major Blackwall.

A group of children taken at the Rectory about 1955. Back row left to right: David Watson, Sonia Dean, Jenny Mart, Kath Stafford and (possibly) Vernon Belfield. Front row left to right: Philip Slack, Gillian Roper, Daphne Sherrin, Christine Kinder, Gillian Wheeldon and Jane Greengrass.

Wakes Queen and her attendants taken in the Rectory Garden in the 1950s. Back row left to right: Irene Hall, Joan Whittaker, Betty Hallows, Jean Whittaker and Margaret Booth (née Cooper). Front row left to right: Ann Slack, Carol Freeman, Doreen Hallows, Marlene Ward and Barbara Goodhead.

The Reverends Richard Smith and Robert Caney at the Church Garden Party at Blackwall in about 1985.

Trinity Folk making the tape *We Will Sing* in Church in 1989. Left to right: Mike Kirk (assisting with the recording), Matthew Spencer, Robert Spencer, Sophie McBride, Mark Rigby-Jones, Victoria Mitchell, Sally Addison, Laura Wilton, Jane Rigby-Jones, Lucy Holmes, Lisa Kirk, Claire Holmes, Robert Tatham, Jan Walding and Jim Addison.

Peak Practice 'bride and groom' leaving the church, Dr Jack Kerruish (Kevin Whately) and Dr Beth Glover (Amanda Burton) in 1994.

Kevin Whately outside Greenbank with village children who became the choir for the wedding. Left to right: Katie-Belle Smith, Ian Matkin, Laura Jones, Robert Spencer, Sarah Jones, Andrew Newsham, Katie Blake, and Becky Walding.

Methodist Chapel

The story of the Methodists in Kirk Ireton is a story of three chapters and two buildings. The chapters could be called 'The Foundation Years', 'The Middle Period' and 'The Continuation'. The foundation years cover the period from 1830 to 1876, the middle period stretches from 1877 to 1983, and the continuation is that unfinished period starting in 1984 when the Methodists returned to their original chapel.

The first building, on Windy Close off Windy Hill and north of the 'free quarry', formed the old portion of the building we know today on the west side of Coffin Lane. Negotiations for the site, owned by a butcher, William Miles, appear to have started in 1830. An indenture agreeing the sale of the land, 64 yards, was agreed in 1836. The deed was drawn up by a Mr Howarth, representing a Wirksworth firm of solicitors. The document was signed by William Miles and the Trustees of the Methodist Church: Samuel Heaton farmer, of Gibfield, Charles Wood footman, of Blackwall, Isaac Raines husbandman, of Kirk Ireton and William Lowe carpenter, of Hognaston. Thomas Peat shoemaker, made his mark with a cross. The purchase price was £6. The opening of the chapel in 1836 is recorded above the original door that opens onto the lane.

The original chapel showing the addition on the left constructed in 1984.

Information about the Methodists and their chapel is then missing for some 40 years. The next information we have is from the Chapel's Trustees Meetings Minutes Book of 1875–1925; the entry for April 15 1875 is concerned with the purchase of land for the new chapel. The entry records that at a Trustees meeting a resolution was passed to 'Purchase title of land off Mr Joseph Matkin for the sum of £12'. The land, formerly gardens, '...measuring two hundred and eighty seven yards and a half, more or less' lay almost opposite the original chapel on the east side of Coffin Lane. The cost of the Chapel 'should be not greater than £350, and that the cost, if possible, should fall between £300 and £350'. The Conveyance, again drawn up by Mr Howarth is dated May 13 1875.

A Mr Kerridge of Wisbech, was approached to draw up plans and a specification for the building. These were directed to cost between £2 and £2.10s. These costs could not be met immediately and Mr Dean the Treasurer, Mr Rains the Secretary and Mr Hoon, assistant secretary formed a committee 'to write begging letters for subscriptions'. Finance for the new chapel was largely donated by the members but a lecture 'The glorious revolution of 1688' also provided some income as did pew rents. An entry for 1875–77 shows that the chapel's expenditure was £559.0s.11½d and the remaining debt £150. Repairs to the structure and purchases such as that of an American Organ, from a Grantham church, ensured that, despite all efforts, the chapel still had a debt in 1899.

The following records of expenditure between 1886 and the 1930s make interesting reading especially as regards inflation during this period:

1886	Organist's services for the year	£2. 0s. 0d.
1927	Organist's services for the year	£2. 0s. 0d.
1880	Oil and candles	14s. 6d.
1886	Oil and candles	13s. 5d.
1886	Chapel cleaning	£3. 0s. 0d.
1932	Chapel cleaning	£4.10s. 0d.
1919	Postage stamps	1s. 3d.
1938	Electric light bill (1st quarter)	13s. 3d.
1938	Electric light bulb	1s. 6d.

Other items on the shopping list during these years included: flannel, soap, soda, whiting, blue, lamp wicks, lamp glasses and brushes. Coal and coke were regular items of expenditure but the quantities were not recorded frustrating efforts at price comparison. Perhaps it was such omissions that led to the first auditing of accounts in 1896?

We have been able to record two tales of Methodist characters, Mrs. Roper (nee Wright) and Samuel Woods.

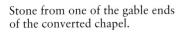

Mrs. Roper who was the chapel organist 'for years and years': '...she'd come down street to play organ, hat under one arm, pins in mouth and she'd run down and roll her long hair round and round, stick pins thro' it and stick her hat on and run off to chapel'.

Of Samuel Woods '...he was the Sunday School teacher for the Chapel. He used to come down through the fields off the Top Lons (Peat's Close) through the Flatts as we used to call it then. He used to come with his prayer book, reading all the way down the footpath. He used to come twice a day, in the morning and then again in the afternoon and many a time he came three times a day to that chapel. It was always full and he was a religious fellow'.

Stone from one of the gable ends of the converted chapel.

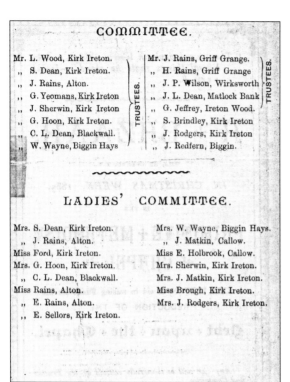

COMMITTEE.

Mr. L. Wood, Kirk Ireton.	Mr. J. Rains, Griff Grange.
„ S. Dean, Kirk Ireton.	„ H. Rains, Griff Grange
„ J. Rains, Alton.	„ J. P. Wilson, Wirksworth
„ G. Yeomans, Kirk Ireton	„ J. L. Dean, Matlock Bank
„ J. Sherwin, Kirk Ireton	„ G. Jeffrey, Ireton Wood.
„ G. Hoon, Kirk Ireton.	„ S. Brindley, Kirk Ireton
„ C. L. Dean, Blackwall.	„ J. Rodgers, Kirk Ireton.
„ W. Wayne, Biggin Hays	„ J. Redfern, Biggin.

(TRUSTEES.)

LADIES' COMMITTEE.

Mrs. S. Dean, Kirk Ireton.	Mrs. W. Wayne, Biggin Hays.
„ J. Rains, Alton.	„ J. Matkin, Callow.
Miss Ford, Kirk Ireton.	Miss E. Holbrook, Callow.
Mrs. G. Hoon, Kirk Ireton.	Mrs. Sherwin, Kirk Ireton.
„ C. L. Dean, Blackwall.	Mrs. J. Matkin, Kirk Ireton.
Miss Rains, Alton.	Miss Brough, Kirk Ireton.
„ E. Rains, Alton.	Mrs. J. Rodgers, Kirk Ireton.
„ E. Sellors, Kirk Ireton.	

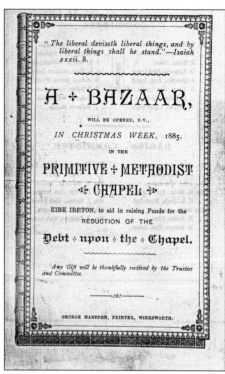

"*The liberal deviseth liberal things, and by liberal things shall he stand.*"—*Isaiah xxxii. 8.*

A ✛ BAZAAR,

WILL BE OPENED, D.V.,

IN CHRISTMAS WEEK, 1885,

IN THE

PRIMITIVE ✛ METHODIST ✛ CHAPEL ✛

KIRK IRETON, to aid in raising Funds for the

REDUCTION OF THE

Debt ✛ upon ✛ the ✛ Chapel.

Any Gift will be thankfully received by the Trustees and Committee.

—:o:—

GEORGE MARSDEN, PRINTER, WIRKSWORTH.

Above: Details of fund-raising event at the Chapel in 1885.

Left: The Chapel shortly after being sold for conversion to a house in the 1980s. Note the railings, removed for restoration, have since been replaced.

PRIMITIVE METHODIST PREACHERS' PLAN.
ASHBOURNE CIRCUIT, 1892.

"He that spared not His own Son, but delivered Him up for us all, how shall He not also with Him freely give us all things?"—Romans viii. 32.

PLACES. "Blessed are your ears, for they hear."	Time.	JULY. 3	10	17	24	31	AUG. 7	14	21	28	SEPT. 4	11	18	25
Young People's Services	2.45	47	6A	1	7Q	11	41c	31	8E	1	15E	1	42G	7H
Ashbourne	6.30	47	6A	1L	7Q	11	41c	31	8E	1s	15E	1	42G	7H
Monday	8		1			1R	1		1*		1		1	1
Friday, Band of Hope	7													
Kniveton	2	10CM	19	20A26	42	1Q	9	8	ss	44	1E	4 24	10	34H
	6.30	10L	19	26A20	42	1Q	9	8	ss	44	1E	14 24	10	34H
Tuesday	7		1			1R			1*		1s			
Hognaston	2	17	53Q	2224	48A	8	11	1E	51	7CM	47	ss	43	1H
	6.30	17	53Q	2224	48A	14	11	1E	51	7L	47	ss	43	1H
Thursday	7		1			1R			1Wd			1s		
Kirk Ireton	2.15	8CM	42	51A	1	37Q	38	c	10	52E	7	30G	1	H
	6.30	8L	42	51A	1s	37Q	38	c	10	52E	7	30G	1	H
Wednesday	7		1			1R			1*		1 Mo			1
Hollington	2	1A	2125	7CM	45	43E	2026	10G	49	6Q	19	c	23	35H
	6.30	1A	2125	7L	45	43E	2026	10G	49	6Q	19	c	23	35H
Wednesday	7		1s			1R					1			
Hulland	2.30	9E	22	17CM	44	10A	5	47Q	18	19A	16	c	32	11H
	6.30	9E	22	17L	44	10A	5	47Q	18	19A	16	c	32	11H
Thursday	7	1s			1R				1*				1	
Brailsford	2	c	7CM	49	19A	9	1E	32	35Q	17	20G	2126	22	6H
	6.30	c	7L	49	19A	9	1E	32	35Q	17	20G	2126	22	6H
Tuesday	7		1		1		1R			1			1	
Biggin	2.30	19A	32	21E	16	7CM	22	23Q	20	25a26	9	10G	18	15H
	6.30	19A	32	21E	16	7L	22	23Q	20	26a25	9	10G	18	15H
Monday	7			1R					1*					
Tissington	2.30	16	1R	11		21E	16	24	50Q	49		10		10H
	6.30	16	1E	11	6L	2125	46A	14	50Q	43	ss	19	7	10H
Monday	7			1R				1*			1s			

"We preach Christ crucified." Preachers & Residences.

1 T. RANDALL...Mayfield Road, Ashbourne.
2 R. Lee.............Hognaston.
3 S. Dean............Kirk Ireton.
4 R. Rowbotham.......Kniveton.
5 G. Woolley.........Hulland.
6 J. Rains...........Kirk Ireton.
7 G. Wigley..........Kniveton.
8 J. Bembridge.......Hognaston.
9 T. Botham..........Tissington.
10 J. Fearn.............Ashbourne.
11 W. Wright............Tissington.
12 G. Hoon.............Kirk Ireton.
13 W. Coxon............Ashbourne.
14 A. Dakin............Ashbourne.
15 T. Beeston..........Hognaston.
16 T. Jackson..........Ashbourne.
17 J. Redfern............Biggin.
18 G. Clowes...........Ashbourne.
19 J. Broom............Ashbourne.
20 Jno. Rains.........Kirk Ireton.
21 Jos. Rains.........Kirk Ireton.

On Trial.
22 T. Beeston, jun....Hognaston.
23 T. Webster.........Hognaston.

Candidates.
24 F. Wright..........Tissington.
25 H. Witham.........Kirk Ireton.
26 S. Wood...........Kirk Ireton.

Auxiliaries.
27 J. B. Taylor.......Brassington.
28 J. Bridgett.........Holloway.
29 W. Beardsley.......Ashbourne.
30 J. Walker..........Bolehill.
31 J. Insley..........Ashbourne.
32 J. Miller............Weston.
33 W. Meakin..........Ashbourne.
34 H. E. Hinge........Ashbourne.
35 J. Kenderdine.....Brailsford.
36 J. W. Beeston........Belper.
37 J. Starkey........Wirksworth.
38 J. Storer.........Wirksworth.
39 J. Fearn..............Winster.
40 J. Smith.......Ireton Wood.

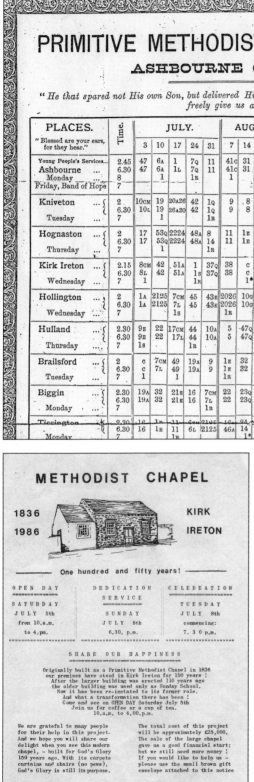

METHODIST CHAPEL

1836
1986

KIRK IRETON

One hundred and fifty years!

OPEN DAY	DEDICATION SERVICE	CELEBRATION
SATURDAY JULY 5th from 10 a.m. to 4 p.m.	SUNDAY JULY 6th 6.30 p.m.	TUESDAY JULY 8th commencing: 7.30 p.m.

SHARE OUR HAPPINESS

Originally built as a Primitive Methodist Chapel in 1836 our premises have stood in Kirk Ireton for 150 years! After the larger building was erected 110 years ago the older building was used only as Sunday School. Now it has been re-instated to its former role. And what a transformation there has been! Come and see on OPEN DAY Saturday July 5th Join us for coffee or a cup of tea. 10 a.m. to 4.00 p.m.

We are grateful to many people for their help in this project. And we hope you will share our delight when you see this modern chapel, – built for God's Glory 150 years ago. With its carpets curtains and chairs (no pews), God's Glory is still its purpose.

The total cost of this project will be approximately £25,000. The sale of the large chapel gave us a good financial start; but we still need more money! If you would like to help us – please use the small brown gift envelope attached to this notice.

150th Anniversary of a Methodist Chapel in the village.

3

The School

Education of children in Kirk Ireton dates back over 300 years. In 1686 John Slater left in his will 'five closes' called the Nether Field and Blackwall Flatt from which the rents of £8 per annum were to be paid to the school master for the instruction of 16 poor children of Kirk Ireton. Other benefactors left legacies for the education of the village's children and the poor, including John Bower in 1744 and Robert Cooper in 1782. It is thought the original school building was off Main Street not far from the current school site.

Although it is not known when the school moved to Well Banks the log books begin from there in 1872 and its position is recorded in that location on the Ordnance Survey Map of 1880. The relatively small building consisted of two parts, the boys on the ground floor and the girls and infants above. The 'offices' for the boys were across the road, available for the use of anyone who cared to use them. By 1881 the School Inspector was already criticising the conditions, saying, 'Upon my visit the temperature two yards from the fire read 44 degrees, the children shivering frequently with cold. The seats are hard. Loose wooden planks on iron supports with no back to lean on unless they are fixed to the cold damp walls.' The School Inspectors threatened to withhold funds and even close the school unless the premises were improved.

Children playing beside the well on Well Banks below the old school. It can be seen that the building was larger then than it is now.

An entry from the school logs in 1875 shows an example of how some parents paid for their children's education. 'Mrs Wright came and made a great disturbance at the school about her daughter Sarah Jane having to pay 3d per week instead of 2d, the former being the fee the children in Standard III pay and in which her child has been since last inspection. The woman said she would not pay the extra penny and wanted her daughter to be put back to the 2nd Standard again which I told her would not be. Having stated the case to the Rector he ordered me to send the girl home for the money on Monday next.'

In 1882 the School moved to the current site on Main Street and the boys and girls schools were merged in the 1890s. Although the cramped conditions had improved, little else had. On January 8 1894 the Girls School Log records 'On arriving at school this morning I find the floor in a thoroughly damp condition, in fact many parts of it are covered in ice. We scraped off as much ice as possible and left a good fire hoping to begin work the next day.' The entry of the 9th reads 'Another attempt to re-open school but impossible as the pipes have burst.'

Extracts from school log of 1872.

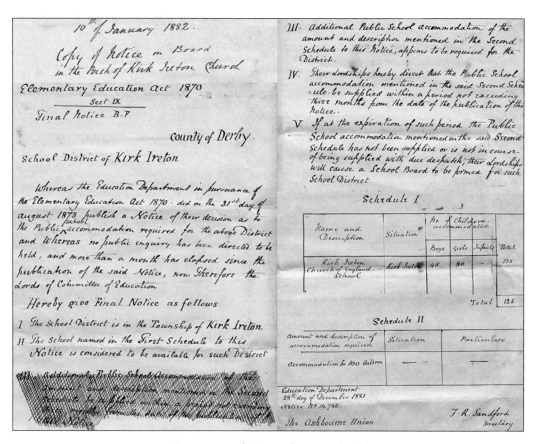

Documents relating to the new school.

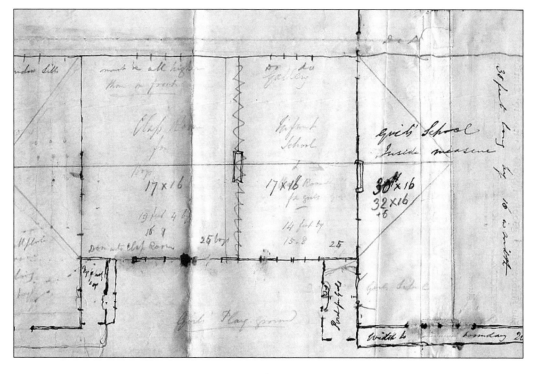

Boys' School. " The results of the Examination are creditable to the Master. It is much to be wished that the new School-rooms may soon be available."

Girls' School. " The Reading and Writing are poor. The Arithmetic is very poor. The Infants are backward."

Very much better results of instruction will be expected next year in the Girls' School (Article 32 (B).

The Scholar numbered 35 on the Girls' School Examination Schedule, having been returned last year as over six, was disqualified by age for further presentation under Article 19 (B)1.

None of the Scholars for whom Honour Certificates are claimed, satisfy the requirements of the Regulations applicable thereto.

NOTE—The subject (if any) specified after each Candidate's or Pupil Teacher's name denotes that the result of the examination therein has been *unsatisfactory*, and that improvement will be looked

School logs from 1880.

List of Subscriptions.

	£	s.	d.
Rev. W. Hombersley	50	0	0
H. W. Walthall, Esq.	100	0	0
Rev. C. and Mrs. Evans	100	0	0
Miss Evans	20	0	0
Miss v. Frantzius	5	0	0
The late Lord Geo. Cavendish	5	0	0
Basil Woodd, Esq.	10	0	0
Mrs. L. Woodd	20	0	0
I. B. Evans, Esq.	10	0	0
Mrs. Blackwall	10	0	0
Miss Blackwall	1	0	0
Master J. E. Blackwall	1	0	0
Miss Evelyn Blackwall	1	0	0
Master R. M. Blackwall	1	0	0
Master W. A. Blackwall	1	0	0
T. W. Evans, Esq., M.P.	2	0	0
Mrs. Gadsby	2	0	0
Sir H. Wilmot, M.P., V.C.	1	0	0
Mr. Dean, Barley Mow	5	0	0
Mr. Harvey	5	0	0
Mr. Heathcote	5	0	0
Mr. John Matkin	5	0	0
Mr. Joseph Matkin	5	0	0
— Geo. Bown	4	0	0
— D. Pickering	3	0	0
— T. Winson	2	0	0
— C. Wood	1	0	0
— Key	1	0	0
— Dronfield	1	0	0
Mrs. Eaton, Nuttall	5	0	0
Mr. J. Slater	5	0	0
— John Cooper	1	0	0
— Job Redfern	0	10	0
— George Smedley	0	5	0
— Joseph Smedley	0	3	0
— Jacob Smedley	0	2	0
Miss Heathcote	1	0	0
Mr. Thos. Taylor	0	10	0
Mrs. Ford	0	2	6
— Smedley	0	1	0
— Heaton	0	2	6
— Woodhouse	0	2	0
— Joseph Wright	0	5	0
Mr. George Hudson	0	1	0
— George Brown	0	2	0
— Joseph Winson	0	5	0
— John Hodgkinson	0	1	0
Mrs. Stafford	0	1	0
Mr. W. Doxey	1	0	0
— John Brown	0	2	6
— James Cockayne	0	5	0
— Henry Cockayne	0	1	0
— J. Whittaker	0	3	0
— L. Wood	0	2	6
— John Allsop	0	5	0
— John Allsop, Junior	0	5	0
— W. Dean	0	5	0
— Jas. Simpson	2	0	0
— Henry Ward	0	2	6
— Daniel Doxey	0	1	0
Mr. Chas. Wrightson	2	0	0
— J. Bartholomew	0	10	0
— Henry Millington	0	5	0
— Henry Leason	0	5	0
— R. Taylor	0	2	6
— Jas. Ward	0	2	6
— S. Greatorex	0	2	6
— Joseph Beeson	0	5	0
Mrs. Smith	0	1	0
Mr. George Hoon	1	0	0
Miss Slater	0	5	0
Mrs. Repton	0	1	0
Dr. Broster	1	0	0
Mr. S. Repton, Junior	0	2	6
— Goodacre	0	2	0
— Talbot	1	0	0
— Geo. Ford, Junior	0	2	0
— John Ward	1	0	0
Mrs. Ford	0	1	0
Mr. Thos. Greatorex	0	2	6
— Geo. Warren	1	0	0
— E. Bromley	0	0	6
— Geo. Wright	1	0	0
— Robert Steeples	1	0	0
— John Hall	0	2	6
— John Morley	0	1	0
— John Ward (Thornley)	0	1	0
— John Ford	0	1	0
Miss Pickering	0	1	0
Mrs. Yeomans	0	1	0
Miss Yeomans	0	1	0
Mr. John Matkin, Senr.	0	2	6
— Henry Ford	0	1	0
— George Harrison	0	5	0
Mrs. Harrison	0	1	0
Mr. Robert Bains	1	0	0
— Isaac Dean	1	0	0
— Geo. Ford, Senior	0	5	0
Miss Ford	0	3	0
Mrs. Simpson	0	1	0
Mrs. Millington	0	1	0
Mrs. S. Millington	0	2	6
Mr. John Ward, Shoemaker	0	2	6
Mrs. Dean	0	2	0
Mr. George Fearn	0	1	0
Mrs. C. Kinder	0	1	1½
Mr. John Ford, Bolehill	3	0	0
— Geo. Slater	2	0	0
— Wallbank	0	10	0
— O. Crofts	0	1	0
— Howe	3	0	0
— Wm. Downing	5	0	0
— M. G.	3	3	0
Mrs. Budworth	0	10	0
J. P. Sheldon, Esq.	0	10	0
Mr. George Woolliscroft	2	0	0
Mrs. Woolliscroft	1	0	0
Mr. Allen	0	10	0

Kirk Ireton Schools.

✠

The present Building being found inadequate for the wants of the Parish, and the requirements of Government ; badly situated also as regards play-ground and other conveniences—advantage has been taken of the offer of premises in the centre of the village, and on a most eligible site, which have been purchased for the sum of £600, and may be converted into excellent Schools at a further cost of £400 to £450.

Until the purchase money is raised, to pay off which it is proposed to have a sinking fund, and a separate account, there will rest a mortgage on the building that will seriously interfere with the income of the Schools.

A Building Committee has been formed, by whom this appeal is issued, to solicit the voluntary contributions of the owners of property, and of the parishioners generally to this most necessary and worthy object.

(Signed) W. HOMBERSLEY, *Chairman.*

C. EVANS,
J. B. E. BLACKWALL,
SAMUEL DEAN,   } *Sub-Committee.*
MOSES HARVEY,
GEORGE BOWN,

February, 1882.

Contributions will be thankfully received by the Rector, Members of the Sub-Committee, and at the Wirksworth Banks.

List of subscribers to the purchase of the site of the new school.

Children outside the new school, possibly at its opening in 1882.

An example of a school timetable. The school was divided into Standards I to VI and the children taught by teachers, pupil teachers and monitors. Although there were strict timetables, absences, not always through illness, and school closures were common. Examples of absences recorded in the school logs include 'Farmers being busy with the hay many children have been absent from school (31 boys away all week)'; 'I hope the attendance will be better when the potatoes and turnips are lifted'; 'Attendance poor owing to boys engaged in gathering sticks'; 'Very poor attendance – many of the older girls being kept at home to assist in spring cleaning'; 'Children engaged in gathering coltsfoot and cowslip flowers.'

Above: The school showing the bell tower on the roof. It is recalled that the headmaster, Mr Abell, rang the school bell by pulling a rope that hung through a hole in the classroom ceiling. In 1917 the bell tower was described as being in a dangerous place and it was moved to the playground, where it remains today.

Left: An example of an attendance register from 1887.

NAME Place Surname first	Age on LAST birthday	Reading	Writing	Arithmetic							Under what Standard NOW examined	Number
Brought forward...												
Slater Isaac	10										I	51
Millington Samuel	9										II	52
Leason Walter	9										"	53
Leason Arthur	9										"	54
Yomans Arthur	8										"	55
Holmes John T.	8										"	56
Dovey Alfred	8										"	57
Jeffery Hugh B.	10			E							"	58
Wood George (b)	12	o	o	V							"	59
Ford John Wm	11			E							III	60
Hodgkinson Charles	9	o	o								"	61
Jeffery John Wm	9½	o	o								"	62
Knight Frank	9		o								"	63
Warren Frederick	9										"	64
Warren Robert	10		o								"	65
Johnson Robert	10										"	66
Cockayne Frederick	9	o	o								"	67
Brindley Thomas	10		o								"	68
Wilson William	10										"	69
Elliott Walter	9										"	70
Smedley Jacob	9										"	71
Smedley Frank	9										"	72
Ward Arthur	10		o								"	73
Staples William	10										"	74
Repton Charles	11										"	75
Allbank James	11										"	76
Dovey Arthur	10										"	77
Lowe James	12	o	o								"	78
Hodgkinson Joseph	13	o									"	79
Yomans Walter	10										IV	80
Cooper Joseph	10										"	81
Cooper George	10	o	o								"	82
Watkin Thomas	12		o								"	83
Cockayne Henry	11										V	84
Ward Harry	12	o	o								"	85
Ray William	11		o								"	86
Pickering Alfred	11										"	87

49

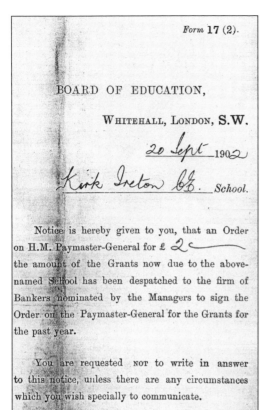

Form **17** (2).

BOARD OF EDUCATION,

WHITEHALL, LONDON, **S.W.**

20 Sept 1902

Kirk Ireton C.E. School.

Notice is hereby given to you, that an Order on H.M. Paymaster-General for £ 2 the amount of the Grants now due to the above-named School has been despatched to the firm of Bankers nominated by the Managers to sign the Order on the Paymaster-General for the Grants for the past year.

You are requested NOT to write in answer to this notice, unless there are any circumstances which you wish specially to communicate.

Grants order with a postmark of 1902.

School accounts 1909.

Left: One of the greatest influences on the school was Benjamin Abell who was Headmaster from 1895 to 1926. He lived at first in the School House next to the school and then moved to Lowton House near the Village Hall. On his arrival he found what he thought to be poor educational standards, untidy handwriting, blots on every page and generally poor learning. In 1896, in an attempt to improve the village's reading standards as a whole, he set up a Library of Penny Books and a Free Reading room, equipped with old magazines and papers. This would open before school started. In the evening he ran a Continuation School that attracted up to 10 older scholars. This incorporated a Recreational Club that met four times a week for reading, draughts and dominoes. Funds were raised to buy a lantern for the students (1897), a lamp to the value of 30s (1898), a free supper (1898) and an air gun 'to encourage students to attend regularly' (value 17/6). He was described as follows: 'He was always dressed in the same grey suit, grey cap and shiny black boots. He was very strict, used a strap, 4 strokes on the hand or rear. The lads cut strips off it on the sly until it was eventually replaced by a hazel cane.'

Photographs of classes (Standards) about 1910.

Mr Abell was responsible for establishing a school garden (now the garden to Stonecroft, Hob Lane) where each boy was given a small numbered plot for which he was responsible. The best gardener was given a silver medal. A former pupil recalls: 'There were no proper gardening classes after Mr Abell left since the lads' knowledge was superior to that of the lady teachers'. Back row, left to right: A. Wanford, J. Jennings, L. Wood, J. Matkin, C. Ford, H. Repton, T. Holmes, S. Roper, J. Cauldwell. Also showing on the front row: E. Smith, J. Smith, H. Ward, T. Smedley, H. Holmes, L. Maskrey and F. Rose.

In the school garden where bee keeping was also taught by Mr Abell. During the First World War the produce was sold and the profits divided between the master and the boys.

Mr Abell with schoolchildren 1912.

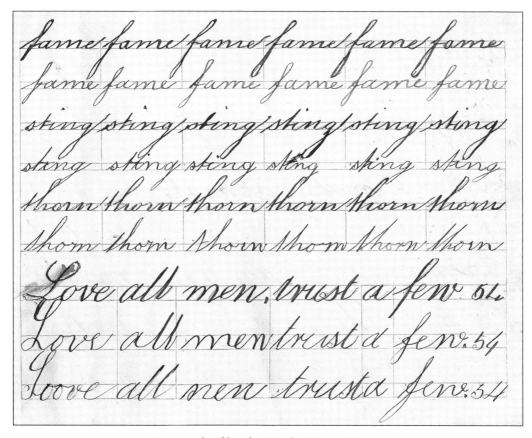

An example of handwriting by George Cooper.

Photograph from 1912 showing Mr Abell on the right and Jessie Archer on the left.

Photograph from about 1912 showing pupils and teachers who are thought to be Jessie Archer on the left and Rose Downing on the right.

'Bathing the doll. We used a large wooden jointed doll and put a nappy on it. This was part of the mothercare classes taught by the school nurse. Miss Jessie Archer was our teacher. She died on October 25 1918 from pneumonia following influenza during the severe epidemic of that year.'

Teacher Miss Jessie Archer. Front row from left to right: Annie Greasley, Cissie Clay, Lily Greasley, Mary Jane Cooper and Evelyn Ward. Back row from left to right: Edith Greatorex, Barbara Greasley, Hilda (Hannah) Ward, Annie Wood, Elsie Smedley, Beatie Smedley, Annie Whittaker, Annie Ward, Katie Sherwin and Ada Morley.

Sewing Class about 1925. Those present include Daisy Ford and Ellen Smith.

Photographs of the schoolchildren in 1912.

School photograph from 1951 showing back row left to right: Ian Cauldwell, Roy Goodhead, Brian Freeman, Bill Hallows, Eric Mart and Solomon Dal? Middle row, left to right: David Watson, David Hallows, Mary Kinder, Monica Ford, Margaret Sherrin, Kath Ford, Mary Watson and ? Hallows Front row, left to right: Ken Greatoex, Colin Sherwin, Rene Moxon, Marlene Ward, ? Stafford, Laura Greatorex, Jane Greengrass, Carol Freeman and ? Brown.

Kirk Ireton Clothing Club.

No._____

_____ _____ 18

£   *s.*   *d.*

Members' Contributions   ....

Added ....

Total   ....

Clothing Club membership card. 'We paid into it at school, once a fortnight. You couldn't pay less than 6d and you could pay more if you could afford it. At the end of the year they reckoned up how much you'd got and they'd give you this ticket and put how much you'd got and a little bit of interest which wasn't much and you took that to a shop. You know where it is in Wirksworth well there used to be a shop there called Sam Land and we used to go there and I can remember going with my club ticket when I first got married I bought a pair of sheets and they were 4/11d.'

Kirk-Ireton C. of E. School. Department Mixed + Infants.

The following pupils are absent (a) suffering from, (b) as "contacts" of the disease mentioned.

Name of Child.	Address.	Disease. Whether (a) or (b).	Class.	Date when last at School.
Batts John Albert	Main Street, Kirk-Ireton	Scarlet fever (a)	I	20/3/45
Smedley Graham	Holly Bush Farm " "	Scarlet fever (b)	I	21/3/45
Cadfield Graham	Town End Cottage " "	Scarlet fever (b)	I	21/3/45
dgkinson Irene	Gate Farm " "	Scarlet fever (b)	II	19/3/45
all Irene	Gate Farm " "	Scarlet fever (b) Infants	22/3/45

(Signed) L. R. Dean (Acting) Head Teacher.
—— 194 5.

Illnesses amongst children included whooping cough, measles, influenza and scarlet fever. The school was once closed for two months due to diphtheria.

A gathering outside the school in the early 1950s. Photograph includes, from back left to right. Mary Watson, Monica Ford, Margaret Ward, Ian Cauldwell, D Hallows, Colin Sherwin, Dennis Watson. John Moxon, Cynthia ?, D Hallows, Paula Blackham, Carol Moxon, Ken Greatorex, Carol Freeman, Marlene Ward. Jonathan ?, Christine Kinder, ?, Mark Hallows, Jennifer Mart, Jane Greengrass, Rachel Stafford, Catherine Stafford. ?, Jo Sherrin, Gillian Roper, Sonia Dean, Phillip Slack, Gordon Mart, Morris Ward.

A country dance set in the 1950s.

May Queen and dancers in front of the school, 1950s.

May Queen and attendants photographed in school, 1960s.

Head teacher Michael Wiser, teacher Miss Cash and schoolchildren early 1970s.

School photograph from 1972. Back row, left to right. ?, Martin Smedley, Patrick Rowland, ?, David Wagstaffe, Stephen Williams, Michael Dale, Andrew Rowland, Stephen Smith, Roland Smith, Ann Ford, Sally Rowland, Michael Wiser (Headteacher). 3rd row, left to right. ?, Heather Brassington, Jennifer Short, Laura Hetherington, ?, Ruth Spencer, Gillian Smith, Louise Hetherington, Irene Matkin, Ingrid Curry, Rachael Billings, Katherine Billings, Alison Rowland. 2nd row, left to right. Jonathan Twigg, Simon Smith, Ruth Williams, ?, Ann Spencer, Sarah Kenny, Emma Short, ? Marina Smedley, Jackie Walker, ?, Brian Pegg, Simon Wiser. Front row, left to right. Stephen Walker, Ian Ford, Nigel Foreman, Barry Clayton, Chris Clayton, Paul Wright, Michael Smith, Graham Foreman, Richard Clayton, Christian Whitehurst.

School photograph from about 1974. Back row, left to right. Mr Bramley, Michael Smith, Richard Williams, Martin Smedley, Ian Ford, Patrick Rowland, Simon Smith, Paul Wright, Jonathan Twigg, Christian Whitehurst, Stephen Walker, Nigel Foreman. 3rd row, left to right. Mrs Haycock, Helen Booth, Sarah Kenny, Marina Smedley, Alison Rowland, Rachael Billings, Irene Matkin, Lynn Jessop, Ruth Williams, Emma Short, Ann Spencer, Alison Morton, Alison Judge, Marjorie Jesperson. 2nd row, left to right. Phyllis Dean (cook), Brian Pegg, Nicholas Whitehurst, Daniel Shawcross, David Morton, Andrew Booth, Marcus Thorley, Keith Twigg, John Williams, Ivor Griffiths, Matthew Williams, Simon Wiser, Allan Potts, David Stevens, Raymond Kenny, Margaret Smith. Front row, left to right. Rosemary Naylor, Rebecca Shawcross, Amanda Booth, Mrs Fuller, ?, Jackie Walker, ?

School Nativity production in Church 1976.

School Football team about 1995, Back row left to right: Jamie Marsden, Jamie Morrison, Oliver Sawyer, Matthew Slack, Andrew Newsham, Ben Slack and Oliver Marks, Back row left to right: Thomas Rogers, Adam Marshall, Will Tomlinson, Matthew Bennett and Charlie Marks.

Children in Victorian costume celebrating the school's centenary in 1992.

Children at the school's Millennium party. Children include, Dan Nolan, Alex Brooks, Shane Spencer, Charlie Lockett, Guy Chambers and Belinda Rowland.

School production 2002. Children include Jenna Ford, Alex Middleton, Amy Booth, Georgia Brooks, Peter Varney, Sorcha Mayes, Miranda Marshall, Mimi Fletcher and Jamie Toms.

At Stanton Bowers on an extended visit, 1988.

Children include, Crystal Holmes, Dan Nolan, Chris Walker, Leah Beardmore, Josh Walker-Thompson, George Tyler, Peter Varney, Kirsty Clarkson, Gemma McGuire, Matthew Fletcher, Charlie Lockett, Caitlin Mayes, Shane Spencer, Joe Middleton, Alex Brooks, Alice Aspin, Ashley Spendlove and Belinda Rowland.

Farms and Farming

4

Despite the generally low agricultural grade of the land around Kirk Ireton farming has provided the main livelihood of the area for many years; even at the time of the Domesday Book there were about 480 acres under cultivation. Ridge and furrow markings in some of the fields indicate that this would have been largely arable farming taking advantage of the relatively frost free areas provided by shelter from hills to the north and west of the village. Today sloping fields and competition, from richer soil areas, have discouraged arable farming in much of the parish but grassy meadows and a plentiful water supply have provided good conditions for dairy farming.

Even into the 1960s there were still as many as nine working farms in the village. The older villagers recall that when they were young, there were cows 'up and down the street all day long,' either moving from field to field or being driven to market. These were all Shorthorn cattle. Farmers turned to Friesians about 1950 as these were more resistant to TB infection and provided a higher milk yield.

Otherfarmers clubbed together to drive their cattle to Ashbourne market every other Thursday but, for Derby market, the cows would be driven to Idridgehay Station and loaded on to cattle trucks. Sheep were only introduced in large numbers after the foot and mouth epidemics of the 1960s and late 1990s.

Farming was arduous work and very routine. Morning and night there would be the familiar sight and sound of the bright shiny churns, each containing 17 gallons of milk, being loaded on to carts and pony traps to be taken to the station. From there the churns were despatched on the milk train to London.

Most of the farmers sold their milk to Nestlés and they would take churns, on trolleys, to the Top Green on Main Street for collection by horse drawn carts. These churns would be returned at eight in the evening for sterilization. This continued until 1933 when wholesalers' lorries replaced the carts and when all milk was sold to the Milk Marketing Board, apart from that sold in jugs from the farmhouse to villagers.

It must be remembered that all milking was done by hand. At most only about 10 cows an hour could be milked and this severely limited the size of herds. Only with the introduction of mechanical milking, which started in the village in the 1950s, did herd size begin to increase. Tractors were introduced towards the end of the war, which made the use of larger ancillary machinery possible. Removal of some hedgerows (also encouraged by government subsidies) to allow manoeuvring of this equipment became inevitable.

In addition to the farms there were many smallholdings where three or four cows and a few pigs would be kept. It has been said that 'During the War everyone had a pig or two.' At one time there were over 30 farms recorded in the village.

The pages that follow are examples of the farms in and around the village.

Church Farm, Wirksworth Road

Church Farm is probably one of the oldest farms in the village. This was modernised in the early 1990s.

The Green Farm, Main Street

The only brick-built farmhouse in the village, this was farmed by Leonard Dean and his family in the 1920s. It has also been occupied by Janet Reger whilst managing her lingerie business in Wirksworth.

Northfield Farmhouse, Main Street

Above: Northfield Farmhouse, Main Street. Isaac Dean farmed here and was later succeeded by his son Stanley.

Right: Stanley Dean and farm workers.

Buxton Hall Farm, Main Street

Dairy door at Buxton Hall Farm, Main Street. This farm was last managed by the Judge family prior to its development as a housing estate in the early 1990s.

Buxton Hall farmhouse before development.

Home Farm, Main Street

Home Farm, Main Street. This farm was one of many originally belonging to Alton Manor. Jos Ford (landlord of the Barley Mow) was farming 28 acres here in 1951.

Home Farm around 1943 showing Trevor Coates and Jos Ford. Trevor was an evacuee to the village with his mother.

Town End Farm, Top Green

Town End Farm, Top Green; the only working farm in the village today. The farm buildings were originally sited behind the Barley Mow. This was one of the first houses in the village to have electricity. The power cables from the quarry at Blackwall went past the farm towards Moorside and on to Wirksworth.

Annie 'Grandma' Dean of Northfields Farm,
Main Street.

Wilfred Dean, haymaking at Millfields Farm.

John Ward on the left with his father George
Ward in the late 1930s.

John Ward on Nether Lane.

Rakestones Farm

Rakestones Farm, Gorses (on the way to Ireton Wood).

Steam thresher at Rakestones.

Upper Hayes Farm, Hayes Lane

Upper Hayes Farm, Hayes Lane. This farm was demolished during the construction of Carsington Reservoir.

Ploughing.

Topshill Farm, Wapentake

Photograph includes Mr Ford, Jack Chadfield, Frank Roper, J. Sherwin, J. Rowland, Cyril Kinder and Stanley Dean.

Alton Hall Farm

Alton Hall Farm. This is a 17th century house; the bay was added for the Walthall family who lived here during the construction of Alton Manor.

John William Ford and his grand-daughters Kath and Monica in 1945 with 'Kit'.

Winneyhill Farm, Hob Lane

Left: Winneyhill Farm, Hob Lane. Valentine Mould is on the left. The family later moved to Durham Farm on Main Street.

Below: The Sitch Farm, Callow. One of the largest farms in the area, it lost acreage to Carsington Reservoir.

The Sitch Farm, Callow

Upper House Farm, Callow

Callow Hall Farm

Callow Hall Farm around 1900. Showing Joe Rowland jnr, Connie Smith, Lizzie Rowland,
Joe Rowland, Pattie Rowland.

Valuation

of Produce Tenantright Fixtures &c on the Callow Hall Farm in the Parish of Callow in the County of Derby, from Mr William Richardson to his landlord H. W. Walthall Esq or his ingoing tenant Mr Joseph Rowland. Made March 21 1899 by Wm Yeomans of Holloway and Brownson & Sons of Derby   Appraisers

Particulars

207	5	3	6	Big Park Leys Growing wheat on Oat Stubble after clover. For the cost of the seed and labor Part manured over. for labor only
34	2	1	38	Wall Close Oat Stubble after seeds mown
208	2	3	30	Little Rushy Meadow Clover root mown
175	3	0	12	The Moor Growing Wheat on Dead Summer fallow. For the usual compensation and for the cost of the seed and labor and for the cost carriage and application of lime applied For labor on soil
170	3	1	39	The Moor
				Part Potato fallow No claim
				" Cabbage land No claim
				" Swede turnip fallow and part common turnip fallow. For rent rates dressings seed and hoeing labor on manure applied less a charge for crop drawn. For ~~dissolved~~ bones as per Agreement of Tenancy
209	4	0	12	Thistly Close Clover root mown For an allowance on the cost carriage and application of lime applied in 1896
194	4	1	12	Harbour Wheat stubble after oats after clover root Now ploughed For the ploughing
196	3	2	0	Big Rushy Meadow Young seeds on Oat stubble. For the cost of the seed and sowing
On Farm				For a quantity of Hedge brushing
				For an allowance on purchased feeding stuffs consumed on the Farm as per Agreement of Tenancy
				Heap of manure Stack of hay
Yard				For 5 heaps of manure

Valuation of Callow Hall Farm from June 27 1892. It is thought that there have been buildings on this site since the 12th century, at one time serving as a monastery with a moat around it. It has been in the Rowland family since about 1900 and was judged the best farm in the County in 1936.

The value of the above written matters and things, after making a deduction for manure made from old produce, we certify to be Two hundred and nineteen Pounds fourteen shillings and ninepence

£ 219 - 14 - 9
15 - 1 ½ stamps &c
218 - 19 - 8

As Valued by the undersigned
William Yeomans
and
Brownson & Son

Received June 27th 1899
William Richardson

Jim Fidler on a bull in the yard, with Josh Kinder.

Haymaking at Callow.

A Ford lorry at the farm. John Rowland is standing on the lorry with Jim Fidler at the front.

Cattle and dairymen in the yard at Callow Hall.

The Hunt at Callow Hall in the early 1960s. Andrew Rowland and his cousin Sally in the foreground.

5 Pubs, Inns and Ale Houses

In the latter half of the 19th century Kirk Ireton had five such establishments, a number comparable with similar communities in other parts of the country. Competition in its various forms has reduced the number. At the start of the 21st century Kirk Ireton has one pub, the Barley Mow. Position was originally perhaps the determining factor involved in the whittling down process; the outlying Windmill, on a high point on Moor Lane to the north of the village (once the site of the Top Holly Windmill, shown on the 1836 Ordnance Survey map, and also allegedly, the site of the village gibbet) and The Gate, on Wirksworth Road, were among the first to go. The Barley Mow, Wheat Sheaf and Bulls Head, all on or adjacent to Main Street, survived into the 20th century. The Wheatsheaf closed soon after the start of the century (1906) and the Bulls Head (after a move from Lowton House at the bottom end of Main Street, to a more central position) nearly saw the century out eventually closing in 1988.

The 'villagers' pub was, up to its closure, The Bulls Head. The domino and darts teams regularly played matches there and were well respected in pubs in the area. The pub was at one time the possessor of 'the best tennis court for miles around'. But it is the imposing Barley Mow, reputedly a former coaching inn and host both to many Foresters feasts in the past and to many committee meetings for all sorts of activities in more recent times, which has survived to the present day.

Quality of the products sold and of the service provided were probably high on the list of other reasons why one establishment was favoured over another. One is tempted to speculate on the effects that the coming, in 1835, of the Primitive Methodist Chapel, with its temperance ideas and later, in 1905, a potable mains water supply, had on the drinking habits of the villagers and the viability of these establishments.

The front of the Barley Mow, Main Street around 1918 showing Lillian Ford leaning on the wall.

Barley Mow

The Barley Mow public house has existed for some 400 years; that is nearly a century longer than the time span from the Fire of London to the landing of men on the moon! Licensed public houses came into existence around 1850 but an ale kitchen or ale house and then an inn has stood on this site certainly since the 1620s although the rear portion, the oldest part of the present establishment, dates from only about 1635–1640.

The home brewing of ale was practised in many homes at this time, indeed it was generally found that drinking ale was a safer method of consuming liquid than drinking water. Even as late as the 1850s, during a cholera epidemic in London's Soho, it was noted that none of the employees of the local brewery suffered from this plague whereas most of the victims drank water from the local pump.

It is, therefore, highly probable that this pub started as a farm house which brewed ale in its kitchen and later developed into an ale house to which the local quidnuncs would go for refreshment and gossip; to make financial and land deals; discuss matters concerning the community; play games such as cribbage, dominoes and darts; and to read, or listen to the reading of newspapers.

The expansion of the business first into an ale house, primarily concerned with the vending of ale, then as a place providing accommodation for both men and horses, led to its transformation into a coaching inn and eventually into a public house of the type we know today.

Architecturally it was quite early on, in 1683 (the date may be seen on the sundial) that today's frontage either replaced an existing timber framed one or was added to the rear portion, at that time a thatched building, to give the present 'T' plan structure. The present entrance door to the bar is thought to have been built between 1790 and 1820. The bar connects to a parlour in the front of the house and to a dog-leg staircase in the north-east corner.

Various alterations to the internal structure have taken place over the years, some to enable a trough for cheese making and a cheese press to be installed. A bathroom was installed over a cellar in the 19th century. On the first floor the two rooms in the rear portion were demolished and a large 40' x 18' room replaced them. This was used as an assembly hall and dining room; probably it was the place that was used by the 'Oddfellows' for meetings and their feasts after which gifts would be distributed to those less fortunate outside the pub. A 'Grand Chamber' existed over the bar on the first floor. Such modifications increased the utility of the building both as a work place and as a meeting place. These changes entailed serious alterations to the structure such as raising the rear roof, demolishing internal walls, moving fireplaces and blocking and moving windows.

The barn at the Barley Mow, now holiday accommodation; note the thatched roof.

Many names well known in the village today have been associated with the Barley Mow in the past, as the following list of landlords since 1750 will show:

1750	John Storer
1753–1759	Ann Storer
1759–1782	John Rowland
1782–1793	Ann Rowland
1794–1805	John Ford
1806–1821	Robert Thornley
1822–1854	Isaac Slater
1854–1884	Samuel Dean (had a 'no smoking' policy – pipes had to be left outside)
1884–1886	Henry Gresley
1886–1938	William Taylor Simpson
1938–1955	Joshua & Lillian Ford
1955–1976	Lillian Ford
1976–	Mary Short

Partly because she was the forerunner of the present landlady, partly because of the long period of time in which she was the landlady and partly because she was 'a character' she is remembered by many of the villagers who have survived her.

Lillian Ann Simpson was born at The Barley Mow on 31st October 1886 the second daughter of William Taylor Simpson whose older daughter, Mabel, had been born in December 1863. Later a brother, James, was born in 1894 but survived for only five months. Lillian lived all her life at the Barley Mow, her age at the time she was photographed in the front garden would have been about 25.

She has been described as having brown hair, large almond shaped eyes, a slightly curved nose and a small mouth with rounded cheeks and chin. Her character was said to be amiable but she was also extremely sharp and would tolerate no nonsense.

As her mother became increasingly infirm Lillian took over the running of the inn. After hours and for many years she was courted by 'Jos' Ford, who lived a stone's throw away in Pebble Cottage (between Blackwall Lane and Top Lons). Eventually Lillian and Jos were married and Jos moved into the pub. Unable to accept Jos as his son-in-law Lillian's father, William Simpson is said to have left in a high dudgeon and went to live with the Miss Deans one of whom (Evelyn) he later married. He came daily to the pub for a glass of beer and to play dominoes but is alleged never to have spoken to Lillian or Jos again.

Lillian kept ducks in the yard and was famed for cooking them. Both she and her mother were highly regarded as cooks and hostesses. It was normal for her to bake biscuits and pass these around the bar. She appears not to have encouraged young ladies to drink in the bar, indeed it was unusual, even in the thirties, to see any women in there, but she did provide tea for them. During the war years some took advantage of the Barley Mow's out of town position to escape from the City, indeed doctors from the DRI were frequent guests.

Outside her pub duties Lillian was church organist for 40 years and also occasionally arranged the church flowers. The choir stalls at this time were lit by paraffin lamps, which she arranged to have converted to the electric lamps seen in the church today. She gave parties in the barn for the choirboys and each year she also had a party for them in the Institute to which she would carry the food she had prepared at the Barley Mow. There was also a gift for those present as they left.

In the final two years of her life Mrs Ford was crippled by arthritis and was unable to move around. Her life became confined to two downstairs rooms. She would sit by the fire in the bar with a biscuit box on her lap containing shillings and florins. Luke Wood, another village character, would draw the drinks and handle the barrels. If you were well enough known and trusted you might be allowed to draw your own drink. You would then go to Mrs Ford who would tell you what you owed and then give change in £ s d; she never converted to decimal currency. It is said that, reputedly like her father who some claim never paid income tax, she ignored VAT. When the Inland Revenue eventually caught up with William Simpson he apparently died so soon after that it was said that 'he died of the income tax'.

Lillian Ford died, 19 years after Jos, working up to within a week of her death on January 26th 1976.

Painting of Lily Ford by Anthony Short.

The Gate Farm Wapentake was one of Kirk Ireton's outlying inns . Villagers recall the sign which welcomed its patrons:

'This gate hangs well and hinders none
Refresh and pay and carry on.'

Site of the Wheatsheaf Inn, Main Street. Elizabeth Ford ran this establishment in 1846 and by 1881 William Garulk was the publican. It remained in existence until 1906 and was replaced by the current building known as 'Laurel Mount'.

Above: Looking east down Main Street with The Bull's Head on the right in the early 1900s.

It seems likely from the 1849 rent charge that the initial site of the pub was 'Lowton House' at the bottom of the village, when William Miles was the occupier. Subsequently the Bull's Head moved to its position half way up the Main Street where it continued to exist until 1982.

Publican George Lowe in the garden to the Bull's Head.

Whereas visitors to the village would have associated the village with the Barley Mow the Bull's Head was very much the villagers' pub.

The village darts and dominoes teams played at the pub. The darts team was a member of the Wirksworth League. Amongst its successes it won The Wirksworth Well Dressing Cup in 1953 and the Ashbourne Carnival Cup in 1960.

Winners of the Well Dressing Cup. Left to right back row: Wilf Ward, Alf Smith, John Yates, Richard Smith, ? Front row: Bill Smith, Stan Smith, Ralph Smedley, Dan Slack.

Above: Doris Kinder presenting dominoes trophies to Mick Stevens and John Ward.

Right: David Stevens being presented with the Arthur Bradwell Dominoes Cup in 1991 by Mrs Bradwell.

The Windmill, Moor Lane. Another of the outlying farms that doubled as an Inn, with William Greatorex recorded as the proprietor in 1849. The 1881 census describes the occupant, Thomas Jones, as a carpenter and joiner so it seems likely that it had ceased to function as an inn by this date.

A notice objecting to the building of Carsington Reservoir was painted on the side of The Windmill.

Out of Hours

Teams and Organisations

When, in 1908, the Rev. Hyde remarked that the premises used for an 'evening club' were not exactly palatial, he noted that 'it could be said to be symmetrical, the holes in the ceiling corresponding with those in the floor.' The walls too, he commented, 'matched the general dilapidation of the whole.'

These observations were to lead, in a year or two, (1910) to the general recognition that the village was in 'urgent need of a parish room' and a committee with Mr Abell, the school head, as secretary was set up to promote the provision of this building. Land, on which two cottages are believed to have stood, was donated by Rev. Hyde and, after the demolition of the cottages, building work commenced.

By 1911 the new Institute had been opened. The Rev. Hyde was fulsome in his praise of the men who built the hall; he praised their conscientious, careful and sound work, their dedication to the work and the fact that although overtime was worked, payment was not asked for, as funds were low. He also highlighted the quality of the materials used in the construction saying 'It might have been put up in the manner of jerry – bad material, badly put together, dear at any price – needing patching in six months and a picturesque ruin in 20 years. The materials are the best. The workmanship is the best. It is cheap because it is good, which is the only cheapness that wise and honest people seek.'

By today's standards the hall was a very basic one; it is doubtful whether initially there was any form of kitchen. There was a ladies' privy (outside against the east wall) but there was no provision for men who, if in need of relieving themselves, went to nearby Rectory Lane. In time, events such as the coming of mains sewerage and electricity, and legislation, e.g. that requiring the provision of disabled facilities, changed both the interior and, to a lesser extent, exterior structure.

The hall was built using local labour and this was undoubtedly one of the reasons for the high standard of workmanship but later this became something of a point of friction in the village. The Rev. Hyde had the hall built as a church hall for church purposes but as time passed church allegiance became less strong and the hall was used increasingly for non-church activities. Mr Abell allowed billiards and dominoes until PC Rose put a stop to them after discovering that gambling (at 1/2d a nap) was occurring. Magic lantern shows also took place. One villager recalled 'I went to one, it was all about OXO and there were this herd of cows and I've never seen such poor old crocks in all my life – I've never eaten OXO since.' Later there developed an undercurrent of feeling that the hall had been built by the villagers and should belong to the villagers. The hall's maintenance was a burden on a church facing increasing maintenance costs. Eventually the hall was sold in 1972 to the parish council whose members, with three other persons, established the form of succeeding Parish Hall committees.

Today, after renovation work in the 1990s and most recently around the Millennium, which involved enhanced heating, lowering the ceiling, providing roof insulation and considerably improved kitchen and storage areas, the hall is a clean, bright building, generally well suited to the villagers' needs.

Above and below left: Photographs of the Village Hall around 1900; note thatched roof.

Below right: Notice of Parish Council meeting from 1882 to discuss transfer of land for the village hall.

A Parish Meeting is
being called to give the
sanction of the Ratepayers
to the Paper that has been
signed as offered –
Revd. C. Evans has already
handed all the Deeds relating
to the new property to the
Rector to be placed in the
Parish Chest, and when
the Parishioners have
transferred the old Schools
and school residence, garden &c.
to Mr Evans, he will give
up the Deed he now possesses
that will make the Parish
owners in reversion of the
house now occupied by the
Master as tenants under Mr
Job Redfern –
Blackwall Novr 13th 1882.

Village Scouts group from 1988. Back row left to right: Ben Horton, Joseph Sawyer, Richard Spencer, Matthew David. Front row left to right: Mark Rigby-Jones, Steven Ford, Anthony Jennings, Steven Neale.

Toddler Group in 1973. Those present include Irene Rowland, Anita Butt, Kath Stevens, Daphne Naylor, Gladys Pegg, Margaret Booth and Noreen Griffiths.

One of Jo Coleman's tap dancing groups. Left to right; Jane Rigby-Jones, Lisa Kirk, Lucy Holmes, Joanne Ward, Claire Holmes, Laura Wilton and Charlotte Greenwood.

Under fives around 1990, withdawn Blake, Jane Jones, Carol Mitchell and Bev Rowland.

Sian Carradice's Dance and Drama Group 1992.

Women's Institute Golden Jubilee in 1983. Left to right, back row: Anita Butt, Jo Coleman, Doreen Ganley (DFWI), Irene Rowland, Betty Hallows, Shirley Aiton (DFWI). Front row: Mrs McIntyre, Mrs Wildman, Mrs Wood, Mrs Slack and Ena Hardwick.

Easter Bonnet competition at Over 60s around 1980. Photograph includes: Dorothy Mart, Mrs Doxey, Mrs Harding, Mrs Wood, Lily Hodgkinson, Val Wright, Elsie Ward, Mrs Slack, Tom Mellor and Nellie Dean.

Over 60s Group in the village hall. Facing window: Alice Ward, Wilf Ward and George Morley. Facing room: Nellie Dean, Stan Dean, Bert Hallows, Edith Hallows, Susan Kinder, Mary Jane Ward, Lucy Cooper, Stanley Cooper, Alfie Bates, Alf Rowland and Arthur Mansfield.

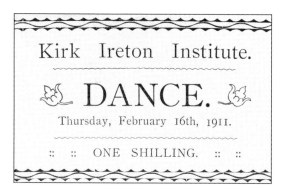

Dance ticket from 1911.

Ernest Smedley jr outside his pigeon loft around 1940.

Singing, dancing, poetry recitals and musical items featured in this event organised by the Kirk Ireton Community Association in 1990. Adults at the back from left to right: Betty and Bernard Hunt, Laura Parry, Ron Middleton and John and Clare Blackwall. Children front row l to r: Laura Mitchell, Amelia Cromack, Lavinia and Charles Blackwall. Children back row left to right: Matthew Spencer, Kelly Rowden, Laura Wilton, Charlotte Greenwood, Vicky Mitchell .... Euan Rowden .... Simon Hills, Adam and Abbie Joyner, Nick Wilton, Laura Kirk and Jonathan Butt.

Christmas Cracker in the Village Hall 2002. Those pictured include Jean Mayfield, Pearl Dunn, Kate Varley, Kath Stevens, Jeremy Butt, Gillian Mann, Susan Fay.

The village held its first Horticultural Show for seven years in 1987. It was staged in the Village Hall and organised by members of the Women's Institute and the Kirk Ireton Community Association. It was so successful that it became an annual event. Back left to right: Mrs Shaw, Mavis Potts, Mrs Lowe, Kate Spencer, Irene Dougan. Front left to right: Matthew, Robert and Richard Spencer.

Visitors enjoying the horticulture show in 1989. Left to right: Susan Grant-Nicholas, Jonathan Grant-Nicholas holding Stacia, Jean Mayfield, Maggie Fieldhouse holding Emily and Jack Mayfield.

Wakes

The patronal festival of any parish church is primarily a religious occasion. In many villages it has for centuries been a local holiday featuring sports and games and an unofficial fête.

The word 'Wake' means maintaining a vigil i.e. walking or watching of the church during the night prior to a holy day. Since the date of the Wakes depends upon the dedication of the church, Kirk Ireton celebrates its Wakes during Trinity week; eight weeks after Easter.

The Wakes at the turn of the 19th century was the highlight of the village year; beginning with the morning Service on Trinity Sunday, followed during the week by sports, racing, dancing, feasting and entertaining friends. The school closed for the week, enabling preparations and celebrations to take place from the Sunday to the Thursday, the latter being the most important day.

The Sunday school celebrated its Anniversary on Trinity Sunday, with two services in the chapel, whilst the Church held special services.

'It was on the Monday evening that Mr Dranfield (the Estates Manager from Alton Manor), who lived in the village at Rose Cottage in Main Street, used to bring out a bucket of monkey nuts and tiny iced gem biscuits to scatter all in the grass outside his house. We children used to scrabble about getting these biscuits.'

On the Wednesday, following a short service in the chapel, there was a free tea party for all the Sunday School children. The tea was served in the Sunday School building, now, once again, the Chapel.

The highlight of the week took place on the Thursday when a procession of clergy, school children, revellers and members of the Honourable Order of Foresters, and of Oddfellows would parade through the streets led by Middleton Town Band.

'The Oddfellows, attired in black suits, white collars and hob nailed boots, and carrying staves decorated with lilies and peonies, were the oldest club so they went first with their banner followed by the Foresters. They'd go to church and walk right round the village and on to Blackwall. In front of Blackwall House the lady and gentleman would come out and speak to them and then the Clubs would come back to the village up in that room over the stables at the Barley Mow. Mrs Ford, the landlady cooked them a dinner. They'd have the largest lump of beef, half as big as a table, and she'd do all sorts of vegetables and they'd have plum pudding and brandy dip... all for 2s 6d.'

In preparation for the Thursday, the fair, sited off Main Street on the Monday, was moved to 'Yards End', now Dean's Field, next to the village field. Here the traditional sports races, Maypole braiding by the school children, bowling for the pig, coconut shy, and duck shoots would keep everyone happy until the evening celebrations began.

Stanley Dean's sisters, Winnie and Elizabeth, were responsible for drilling the Maypole dancers in the 1930s and the annual photograph of the dancers would be taken on the lawn in front of their house .The girls were rehearsed, after school, in the Institute prior to the Wakes. In addition to the dancing, traditional races such as three-legged, egg and spoon, sack, etc. and games of football would keep the children entertained until their free tea was ready.

Villagers' memories of these events are vivid:

'The caravans, most of them still horse drawn, would roll up on the Sunday morning and we children would be there waiting for them.

Old Mrs West would arrive with the donkeys, roundabouts and swing-boats and all the things that went to make a Wakes week – nothing like it is today.' And, 'On the Monday, General Walthall from Alton Manor would place orders at the Barley Mow to give dinner for all his tenants.'

'My mother was the school caretaker and she used to get up that early to get the copper boiler scrubbed out, filled, and a fire made under it ready for Wakes teas. We children had to fetch water from the tap in the street.'

'The Mother's Union made the teas and Mrs Isaac Matkin, from Sitch Farm loaded up a

The procession passing through the village; the Rev. C. Currey with Benjamin Abell on the right.

Above and below: Procession on Main Street around 1900.

washing basket with sandwiches, silver teapots and all cups and saucers. As soon as ever this horse, Bexton, heard Mr Matkin get in the trap, and lift the reins, it used to set off... and it knew where it was going!'

During the war years Wakes Week lapsed but was partially replaced by one-day events largely in aid of the war effort. At one of these a leg of lamb, an unbelievable luxury at that time, was attached to the top of a greasy pole as the prize for anyone who could scale the obstacle. Unfortunately, at lunch time the guardians took their eyes off the pole and the leg of lamb disappeared without realising its full potential. Less spectacular events were organised by the Red Cross such as raffles and teas though the latter, with tea, fats and sugar rationed, must also have had a special appeal.

The Wakes were revived in the 1970s; at first as a weekend event but gradually building up to the event we know today. Stalls, on the verges of Main Street, have often featured; school teas are almost as much a must as Maypole dancing but other events such as village stocks, a ducking stool, Tug of War and wheelbarrow races only really arrived when events became centred on Dean's Field. Lately a marquee has been hired to accommodate the refreshment stalls during the day and dancing in the evening.

The band halts to play outside the Barley Mow.

Alton Manor Estate Manager, Mr Alfred Dranfield, outside Rose Cottage, Main Street with Mrs Jane Dranfield.

Maypole dancing in the 1930s. Maypole Dancing has long been a village tradition, certainly since 1900. Girls wore white pinafores over their own dresses. The older girls made these from 'holland' (a course linen) and decorated with feather stitch. These were worn with black boots and white stockings. Boys wore farmers smocks.

Above: Part of the Wakes procession in 1949/1950 showing Mrs. Coxon and Mrs Wright under window on left; lady with yoke is Mrs. Mileson followed by Mrs. Mart with daughter Jenny (as Mary with her lamb) and Chris Springall and Fred and Cyril Kinder leading the dray.

Right: Maypoling in the 1930s.

Below: Maypole group in the 1950s.

Above: Wakes fancy dress group, 1939, from left: Betty Millington, Lucy Bates, Agnes Dean, John Millington, John Bates.

Left: 'Quads' 1955 Ernie Heathcote, Eunice Coxon, Cyril Ford, Ada Caudwell.

1963 Comic football team Maypole dancing.

Maypole dancing in the 1960s demonstrating the dance 'Gypsy Tent'.

A float typical of the many decorated by the Whittaker family, which they spent many winter evenings preparing. Left to right. Joan, Gladys, Jean, Evelyn, Janet and Sheila.

Wakes procession, Main Street around 1970.

1970s 'Uncle Tom Cobbley' Vernon and Gilbert Matkin leading the horse 'Dolly' owned by Harold Seals, with Rachel, Jennifer and Emma Short. Jennifer (sitting backwards) on horse; also showing pony 'Patchy' ridden by Paul Smith as the Indian brave, led by Tim Snaith.

Circus troupe, those present including Jim, Joan and Sally Addison and Penny and Mike Glendinning.

Wakes Princesses 1984 showing from left to right: Teresa Harvey, Sophie Bailes and Jo Walding.

Fun run from the early 1990s.

Over 60s float from the early 1980s with Tom Mellor, George Morley, Margaret Booth, Dorothy Mart and Beryl Spencer.

Playgroup Snow White, early 80s.

Women's Institute float showing back row from left to right: Irene Dougan, Ena Hardwick and Val Taylor with Irene Rowland and Betty Hallows at the front.

Youth Club Float 1990 with from left to right: Claire Holmes, Ben Morton, Teresa Harvey, Lisa Kirk, Paul Howarth and Sophie Bailes.

Below: Wheelbarrow race down Main Street before the development of Buxton Hall farm on the right.

The school float celebrating its centenary in 1982. Back row, left to right Headteacher Miss. C. Edminson, Gemma Oakes, Richard Spencer, Joanna Butt, Lucy Taylor, Claire Holmes, Tom Morton, Sarah Newsham and Catherine Butt. Front row, left to right, Chris Wiser, James Slack, Anton Howarth, Matthew Slack, Tim Wiser, Kate Oakes, Mark Rigby-Jones, Sarah Oakes, Paul Tatham, and Edwin Morton.

'Uppers and Downers' football teams. 'Uppers' Back Row left to right: Bruce Pollard, Peter Varney, Keith Hall, Neil Smedley, Luke Robotham, Lee Marsden, Will Stafford (hidden), Matt Bennett, Craig Bowyer, Chris Ward and Gary Spendlove. 'Uppers' Front row left to right: Frank Marshall, Rosalie Wood, Ashley Spendlove, Oliver Johnson, George Tyler, Max Marshall, Angus Pollard, Jam Walker, Josh Rowbotham, Christopher Walker, Peter Varney jnr., Cameron Wood. 'Downers' Back Row left to right: James Varney, Steve Ford, S. Manley, Nick Leeman, Philip Marks, Malcolm Pollard, Phil Nolan, Tom Rogers, Charlie Marks, Ed Howard. 'Downers' Front Row left to right: Dan Nolan, Shane Spencer, Jack Torkington and Jack Pollard.

Dr Broster's Pageant showing back row left to right; Lucy Bates, Jean Land and Connie Roland and front row left to right; Sylvia Spence, Dodo Rush and Wendy ?

Dr Broster was a general practicioner in Wirksworth for many years from the late 1890s. His surgery was in a large house by the Station. He has been described as a little man, very strict who was called variously Little Neddy, Little Teddy and Whistling Willie. He wore a smart black suit, spats and a top coat. He had difficult times in his life. He had been a surgeon in the First World War, lost his son in the Second World War, failed to get his anti-communism book published and eventually lost his sight. Despite this he brought a great deal of pleasure to the people of Wirksworth and the surrounding area through his pageants.

He wrote two pageants, the first being produced in 1933. They were called "The soul going over the River Jordan" and "A wood called Pitty" and each had a mythological theme. The actors were recruited from the surrounding villages and Miss Stafford and the village children and adults played an active part. The plays were presented on the Recreation Ground in Wirksworth with Pitty Wood in the background. Money raised from the pageants went towards the purchase of premises in St John's Street Wirksworth to move the local hospital from Babbington House on Greenhill.

'Smithers' the coal man had a solid wheeled Albion for his deliveries. To take villagers to Wirksworth on Tuesdays and Derby on Fridays he would clean his lorry and put 2 benches in. He would come up to the village and put up a step to let people climb on board. 'When you went there'd be pigs, calves in bags and a couple of old hens tied together and butter and all manner of things. You had to shuffle them out of the way to get your feet in'. Websters' busses put an end to these arrangements around 1928. The picture shows 'Smithers' with a group of villagers on an outing to Dovedale in 1924.

Websters bus. Sunday school outing to Eaton Bank, Duffield – early 1940s. Back row, left to right. Janet Morley, Maid, Lizzie Dean, Rev Cecil L Currey, Mrs Manifold (Housekeeper/Maid) Photograph also includes: Gladys Rowland, Phyllis Holmes, Joyce Greatorex, ? Watson, Elsie Kinder, Jean Linthwaite, The Watson sisters, Dorothy Ward.

The Prince of Wales came to the village on 2 June 1932. Doris Linthwaite recalled 'We were all standing outside the school, waving our flags, waiting to meet him, but he didn't speak to anybody. We were very disappointed. He was good looking but so much smaller than I'd expected and seemed very nervous or bored'.

The Prince of Wale at Alton Manor.

Mick Stevens waiting to leave with his bride, Kath Ford.

It has been a longstanding tradition in the village to 'rope the bride'. As the newly wed couple stand at the end of the path to the church, children hold a rope across their way, preventing them from leaving. The groom throws coins onto the road, which the children gather up and then allow the couple to leave.

Above: Everyone from the village assembled on the village green for an official Millennium photograph, taken from an upper floor window of Lavender Cottage.

Preceding Wakes week in 2002 the village celebrated its history in the form of a 'Sound and Light' production. This involved the active participation of about half the village, whether it was in the form of fund-raising, writing, costume making, music or acting. The church was filled for all the shows and the last one ended in a spectacular firework display.

Photograph of Nether Lane looking North with 'ghost'. 'Mud' (Moses) Hudson was a woodcutter and an especially colourful character. It is thought he lived on Nether Lane at one time. He came from a large family, all of whom died from tuberculosis except for Mud. He was 'A very clever chap with beautiful handwriting but nasty; as he passed you never knew if he was going to swear or speak!' He prefixed every sentence with 'Lory to God' and when he was having an argument with his wife neighbours would say 'Oh, it's time for morning and evening prayers!!'.

'I remember going with my mother to fetch a cheese from Hognaston and we carried a 22 lb cheese from there. I wasn't very old so I couldn't do much towards carrying it and my mother were right jiggered when we got home but we thought we were alright 'cos we'd got this cheese in a pillow case! My mother wrapped it in brown paper and put it under the bed.' (Quote from Elsie Ward seen here with her parents Ernest and Libby Smedley and her sister Winifred and brother Ernest jnr.).

Woodcutting was a significant local trade for many years. The men would chop down trees and debark them using a peeling iron. These trees would then be sold to, for example, the Co-op which would take them by cart to Derby.

Sometimes these men would travel to places as far afield as Durham and Gloucester where, in winter, they would go into lodgings, but in the summer they would build themselves a brush covered shelter in a hollow in the woods.

'They had to go by train from Idridgehay Station with saws and the like. They'd perhaps not come home for 6 – 8 weeks at a time. I think it was one of those sort of things that a man had got to be given to before he could do it properly.'

This photograph shows what is thought to be Rose Cottage on Rectory Lane with maids from the Rectory sitting on the wall. Mrs Jennings was the Midwife/District Nurse who lived at Rose Cottage in the 1920s. She would ride a bike or be collected by pony and trap around her area which covered Hulland, Carsington, Idridgehay, Ireton Wood and Hognaston. Her predecessor had walked the district. As well as bringing either pink or blue ribbons to the new baby's house, she would visit poor families and take a pot of jam and a sack of flour to make pasties. Her rate of pay was 10s (50p) for ten days, if she was paid at all.

Daniel Thomas was a Welshman who lived in a tent in Pitty Wood amongst the alder trees. He used the soft white wood to form the soles of clogs, stacking them in careful rows. He worked all hours, and locals were familiar with his lantern bobbing about in the dark. It is thought he lived locally for about 12 years until the alder ran out. He was a learned, well read man who never missed a service at church. He walked down twice every Sunday, used his own Welsh Bible which he carried in the pocket of his black suit and always wore a black bowler, black tie, polished boots, and carried an umbrella and lantern.

Stories vary as to his demise. Some say he was gored to death by a bull, others say he was lost down one of the local mine shafts. 'They couldn't make out why he hadn't come home one night. When daylight came the men of the village went to look for him. His candle was just going out, it was flickering, his clogs were there but he was nowhere anywhere around.'

This story took place during double Summer time. Luke Wood, the church sexton and gravedigger, was asked to dig a grave for a funeral due to take place the following morning. It normally took him a day to dig down the 6 feet of sandstone and soil and it was mostly pick work. On this occasion Luke had been carting hay all day and after milking at 9pm he started to re-open the grave. By the early hours 'I had got the soil out, down to the coffin, a foot each side so it wouldn't go in with me; I heard somebody coming on. I shouted out of the grave 'Eh up, what time is it?'. By gum, he went on that road for Tops'hill so fast and I could hear him running clip clop like a horse. I never knew from that day to this who it was.'

The junction of Nether Lane and Hob Lane. 'And my old Grannie would go off to Church, and she'd got a black skirt with braiding along the bottom sweeping along like a brush. She'd hold it up as if she was going up steps and she'd have this skirt and blouse and all these buttons and buttonholes. Then she'd have a bonnet and she used to look so nice.'

Well Banks before the road was re-routed. The Wright family lived on Well Banks where they kept a collection of musical instruments and would hold musical evenings. They would start with a gallon of beer and then top it up, the sessions lasting for up to three days. It was said that 'Blind Billy' Wright could walk from Kirk Ireton to the Public House at Hognaston, hang his fiddle on a tree when he went over Scowbrook and always find it on the way back.

Above: Well Banks. Sam Cauldwell lived in what is now the demolished part of the schoolhouse on Well Banks. He used to clean at Blackwall House as well as being the night watchman at the quarry. It is said he heard planes overhead one night during the War and switched all the lights on. He used to come home singing hymns and quoting from the Bible. He had a sign up in his window that read 'Duck and ducklings for sale. There's 'owd duck (his wife) and the ducklings have gone'. Another sign said 'One broody hen for sale.'

Above: Emily Constance Dean in her car about 1920. She lived at Vesta Lynn for a while.

Vesta Lynn, Moor Lane. Vesta Tilley was the stage name of Matilda Alice Powles. In the late 1890s/ early 1900s she was England's leading male impersonator. She was a regular visitor to the Mossam family who lived on Moor Lane and they named their cottage 'Vesta Lynn' in her honour.

Pebble Cottage, Blackwall Lane. Frankie Binley lived at Pebble Cottage on Blackwall Lane and was nicknamed 'Polar Bear' because of his beard and his large build. He owned two donkeys and he would turn them out at night so they could feed where they liked. He also owned 3 or 4 cows which he kept in a shed on Well Banks. He would milk them sitting on the side of Main Street where the 'phone box is now. He was the coal merchant and would collect the coal from Idridgehay Station and load it onto his donkey cart. He would set the donkey off walking up the hill, call in at the Barley Mow, have a pint and then catch up with the donkey. The story goes that one day some boys took the donkey off the cart, put it the other side of a narrow gate to a field and then hitched it up again. Frankie could not figure out how the donkey got in there with the cart.

Arthur Dranfield, the Estate manager at Alton Manor, lived at Rose Cottage, Main Street, shown above. He always walked with a stick which he called 'Smiler'. Children of the time remarked that "he didn't mind giving you some either!".

I can remember when we were small, one Saturday he went up the village and he shouted 'Eh, you children, go back and ask your dad if he'll take me a tooth out. Tell him I'm crazy with toothache.' It made our day to see old Dranfield having a tooth pulled out. Me father had to get his old tool bag, go round and round in the bottom of his bag 'til he found these old tooth drawers. 'Open your mouth – which one is it?' We children were all round his chair, watching as he was shouting, long before he got these tooth drawers in his mouth. He was shouting his head off 'Has gor 'im Jack, has gor 'im?' 'Aye, 'ees here, look you' and there was an old tooth stuck on the end of these tooth drawers.

✠ RULES ✠

OF THE

KIRK IRETON ASSOCIATION

Admission of Members.

RULE 1.—Before any person shall be admitted into this Association, he or she shall be proposed at a General Meeting, or at a Committee Meeting, and be elected by the majority present.

RULE 2.—That each member shall pay his or her proportion of the expenses of the Association; and shall agree to observe all the Rules, Orders, and Regulations, and also any Bye-laws which shall be made at any General Meeting, or at any Special General Meeting of the Association.

RULE 3.—That every member of this Association shall continue to be a member, and be liable to bear his or her proportion of the expenses that shall have been incurred, until he or she shall have given a written notice of his or her intention to withdraw, to the Secretary of the Association, two calendar months previous to the Annual Meeting in any year, from which time his or her obligation shall cease, on his or her arrears being paid up to the Treasurer.

3

KIRK IRETON,   188

SIR,

   I beg to inform you that the Annual Meeting of the Kirk Ireton Association for the Apprehension and Prosecution of Felons, will be held on Easter Wednesday the   day of   inst., at the Barley Mow Inn, Kirk Ireton, when your presence will be esteemed a favour.

I am, Sir,

Yours truly,

SECRETARY.

DINNER ON THE TABLE AT TWO O'CLOCK.

It is not known that crime was a particular problem in the village but evidently villagers were prepared if there was any.

Right: Sergeant Major Leverick was the village policeman prior to PC Rose who was the constable in the 1920s. PC Rose lived at The Hollies on Main Street.

129

Left: Edwin Greasley was a special constable with Stanley Dean (above) in the 1940s. Stanley also was a Parish Councillor, a school governor, Parochial Church Council member and Church warden. On Sundays he rang three of the Church bells by himself by using both hands and tying his foot through the bell rope of the third.

In the haycart .The picture includes, from L. Harold Ward, Ron Mould, Ron Smith, Dorothy Ward, John Allsopp. 'He kept me on the farm 'til springtime, happen a full 3 weeks to set cow cabbage'; 3 or 4,000 plants were set in a field for the cows for winter. 'We also went haymaking. On return to school we would get 4 strokes of the strap for not attending.'

Lowton House. After his retirement Headteacher Mr Abell moved into Lowton House where he planted mistletoe and wouldn't divulge how he grew it successfully. It still flourishes today.

Barns at the Barley Mow. The influenza epidemic of 1918 'about cleaned this village out' as it lasted for over six months. Doctor Seals came on horseback from Wirksworth and he would stable his horse at the Barley Mow where he also set up his surgery and 'fixed' his medicine.

View from the Crofts. 'Gentleman' Frank Smedley lived at Fair View on the Crofts during the 1920s. He was a cobbler by trade and was famed for his beautiful garden/allotment on the corner of Hob Lane and Nether Lane.

His brother 'Chocolate' Smedley (whose real name was Wilf) lived in one of the cottages which now forms part of Raglan House on Well Banks. It is not known how he came by the name 'Chocolate'.

'Poacher' Frank Smedley was a trained baker and confectioner but used to spend his time in a shed on the Top Lons, although he also lived on the Crofts. He would sit there all day on a pile of wood shavings but he was hard to see as it is said he sat there with a sack over his head and never spoke or raised his head.

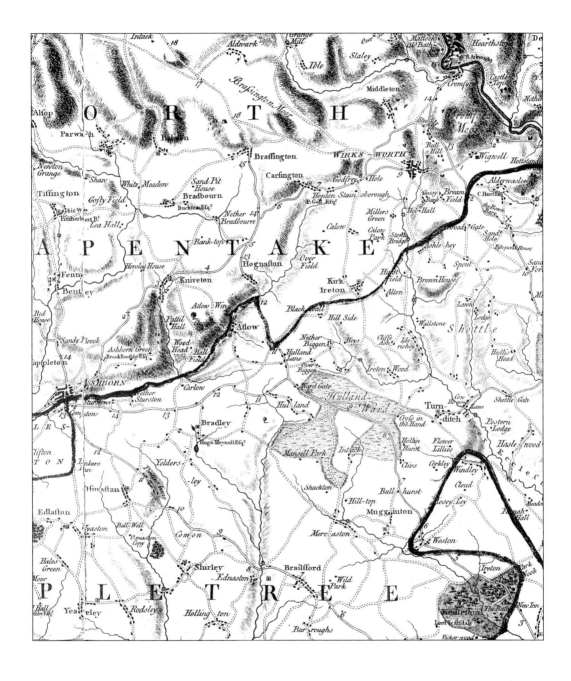

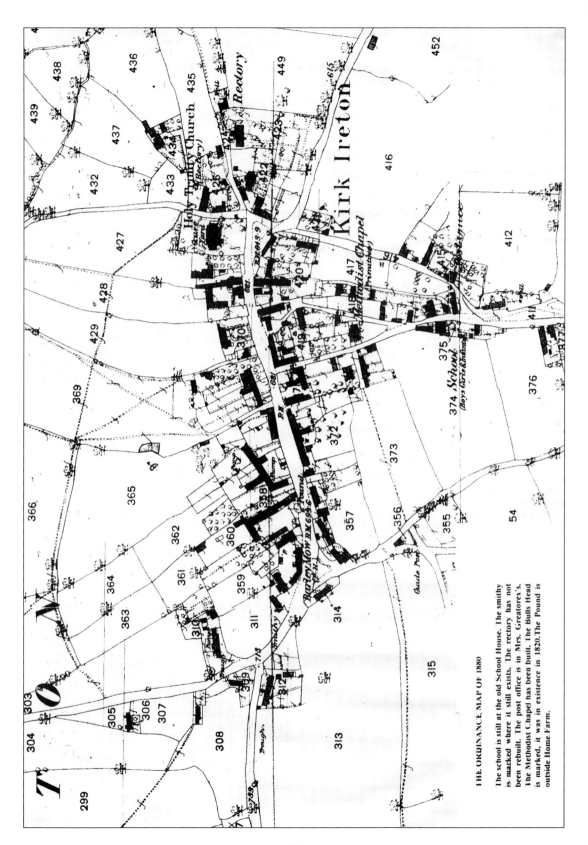

THE ORDINANCE MAP OF 1880

The school is still at the old School House. The smithy is marked where it still exists. The rectory has not been rebuilt. The post office is in Mrs. Greatorex's. The Methodist Chapel has been built. The Bulls Head is marked, it was in existence in 1820. The Pound is outside Home Farm.

The Village Hall on Bottom Green with Greenbank on the left.

Main Street ; note the absence of curbs and street lamps.

Coffin Lane before widening and the construction of the Bakehouse on the right.

Main Street showing Laurel Mount in the foreground.

Above: Seat and pump at Top Green. The pump is situated at one of the original water supply points in the village and is purely decorative. Water was originally collected from two wells on Well Banks. About 1900 two water rams began pumping water to a reservoir on Blackwall Lane which supplied water to taps in the Main Street. Taps were situated at the bottom of the school yard, below the village hall steps, on Main Street, Buxton Hall Farm, at Top Green, on the corner of Gorsey Gate, below the Chapel and at the bottom of Well Banks. There were also wells at Northfield Farm, Churchside Cottage and Green Farm. Kirk Ireton was the first village in the Ashbourne Urban District to receive piped water.

Left: Water spout above the trough on Moor Lane.

Blackwall Lane showing Blackwall Farmhouse on the right and Blackwall Cottage on the left.

The fishpond at Blackwall.

Above: Ralph Blackwall and Mrs Oakdene near Blackwall Farmhouse during the 1930s.

Right: Alf Smith at Blackwall about 1940.

John Ward, Ken
Cauldwell, lads and
horses.

Fred Ford discing
arable land in 1948.

Viv Rowland with
prizewinning shire and
foal.

Right: Snow at Stainsborough (on the way to Hopton) in 1947. Villagers remember 9 consecutive days of snow when nobody went to work because the roads were impassable. Gangs of men cleared the Main Street every day enabling the bread roundsmen to get in, but each night snow drifts formed.

'In the lane to Ireton Wood the snow was over the hedges and children were walking on top of the snow and running their hands along the telephone wires.'

The milk didn't go anywhere; it stayed in the village in improvised storage tanks such as dolly tubs and washing machines.

Below: Main Street in the snow in 1990.

The 'Trig. Point' on The Mountain. This is the lowest hill (242 metres) bearing the name 'The Mountain' in England. The pillar was built in 1938 at a cost of £3 13s 6d. It is, unlike many other pillars around the country, still in use as a navigational aid.

Events have changed the face of the countryside even in the last half century. Above, a stile stands isolated and fulfilling no useful purpose following the post war introduction of grants to farmers for removing hedge rows to facilitate the use of large mechanised farm machinery.

Following the foot and mouth outbreak of 2000 many farmers replaced their cattle with sheep. Stoops, adequate for retaining cattle, were too widely set to enclose sheep and wooden stiles were constructed, alongside the stoops, to help retain them.

Aerial views taken from the Church tower looking west (above) and south (below).